A Course in Basic Writing

A Course in Basic Writing

Susanna K. Horn
Kenneth Pramuk
The University of Akron

HEINLE & HEINLE PUBLISHERS
I(T)P® *An International Thomson Publishing Company*
Boston, Massachusetts 02116 U.S.A.

New York • London • Bonn • Boston • Detroit • Madrid • Melbourne • Mexico City • Paris •
Singapore • Tokyo • Toronto • Washington • Albany, NY • Belmont, CA • Cincinnati, OH

CREDITS
Production Editor   Brenda Owens
Copyediting   Kathy Pruno
Interior and Cover Design   Ellen Pettengell
Composition   Parkwood Composition
Cover Image   Costa Manos, Magnum Photos, Inc.

WEST'S COMMITMENT TO THE ENVIRONMENT

In 1906, West Publishing Company began recycling materials left over from the production of books. This began a tradition of efficient and responsible use of resources. Today, 100% of our legal bound volumes are printed on acid-free, recycled paper consisting of 50% new fibers. West recycles nearly 27,700,000 pounds of scrap paper annually—the equivalent of 229,300 trees. Since the 1960s, West has devised ways to capture and recycle waste inks, solvents, oils, and vapors created in the printing process. We also recycle plastics of all kinds, wood, glass, corrugated cardboard, and batteries, and have eliminated the use of polystyrene book packaging. We at West are proud of the longevity and the scope of our commitment to the environment.

West pocket parts and advance sheets are printed on recyclable paper and can be collected and recycled with newspapers. Staples do not have to be removed. Bound volumes can be recycled after removing the cover.

Production, Prepress, Printing and Binding by West Publishing Company.

 TEXT IS PRINTED ON 10% POST CONSUMER RECYCLED PAPER

British Library Cataloguing-in-Publication Data. A catalogue record for this book is available from the British Library.

Heinle & Heinle is a division of International Thomson Publishing, Inc.

Printed in the United States of America

04   03   02   01   00   99   98   97   8   7   6   5   4   3   2   1   0

Library of Congress Cataloging-in-Publication Data

Horn, Susanna K.
     A course in basic writing / Susanna K. Horn, Ken Pramuk.
        p. cm.
     Includes index.
     ISBN 0–314–20404–0 (softcover: alk. paper)
     1. English language—Rhetoric.   2. English language—Grammar.
   I. Pramuk, Ken. II. Title.
   PE1408.H68347   1997   96–30541
   808'.042—dc20   CIP

Dedication

To Mary King, who brought us into the Writing Lab to work closely with students. And to those students, who have taught us what writers really do.

Every discourse ought to be a living creature; having a body of its own and head and feet; there should be a middle, beginning, and end, adapted to one another and to the whole.

—Plato

Contents

Part 3

Editing   **141**

Part 4

Additional Practice   167

Part 5

Appendixes   185

Foreword—To The Teacher

We contend that students learn to write by practicing writing and getting feedback from their readers rather than by merely completing exercises, no matter how well constructed or creative the exercises may be. Therefore, this volume is intentionally slim, with the expectation that the students' own writing—prewritings, practice sentences, and multiple drafts—will create the course. Although writing is not a linear process, for ease of use, this book is divided into five sections.

Part One: Fluency—the use of expression and focusing exercises to encourage discovery through writing. Students are encouraged to explore their thoughts without regard for correctness, allowing themselves free range to explore their ideas before settling on a focus to examine in detail. At this stage, feedback from peers is essential, both to the development of a sense of audience and as an important way to encourage writer introspection and fluency. Writers will discover that they must revise again and again—until both the audience and the writer are satisfied that the writer's message is complete and is clear to a reader. Because beginning writers are reluctant to believe that all writers struggle, student writing examples demonstrate how other writers use their newly developing skills in the evolution of writing—prewriting, focusing in, and preparing multiple drafts. Only after a writer is satisfied that the ideas in the piece are ready to be presented publicly, does it make sense to attend to correctness at the sentence level.

Part Two: Control—developing control through sentence combining. Students come to a Basic Writing course in college with a repertoire of sentence forms and structures; often this repertoire is more sophisticated than we recognize because students have not learned how to use the techniques of sentence structure as conscious tools for expressing their thinking. This section emphasizes transforming writing from writer-based to reader-based pieces by using student-written sentences to practice coordination, subordination, and the effective addition of details and description. Students also practice each technique either by transforming their own sentences or by composing collaboratively or individually.

Part Three: Editing—editing and proofreading techniques to enhance the textual integrity of a piece of writing. After the struggle to compose is apparently over, the editing begins. All writers know the frustration of not being able to see their own mistakes; therefore, students may benefit by examining the drafts of other beginning writers to discover ways of effectively incorporating the sentence structures they have learned. Proofreading is, after all, a particular way to read a text, a way that helps students pay attention to the surface details that signal literacy to the reader. Reading a draft aloud facilitates recognizing and appropriately marking sentence boundaries, effectively combining sentences, and correctly using internal punctuation.

Part Four: Additional Practice—for reinforcement or review. *Combining Practice* allows students to concentrate on individual sentences as they integrate their sentence combining techniques. *Combining Sentences in a Paragraph* provides opportunity to manipulate sentences within the context of a meaningful piece of writing.

Part Five: Appendixes—an extensive punctuation guide and a concise list of key joining and transitional elements. The appendixes are intended as references for students to use as they compose or edit.

We recognize, of course, that the writing process is undeniably recursive, and we would expect students to be prewriting, drafting, consulting, and revising throughout the entire semester. To this end, many of our Composing exercises refer students back to previous explorations or sentences they have written, emphasizing that writing is never finished. In addition, the Possible Explorations at the end of some sentence exercises suggest further prewriting based on sentences that students have just created. The idea is for students to discover new topics from their own experiences—topics that mean something to them and to their peers.

We do not presume to tell students which topics to draft or which ones to finish. Those decisions are best made by the students themselves. Portfolio requirements we will leave with the instructor, recognizing that the whole concept of a portfolio is a collaborative effort to improve students' writing and to demonstrate that improvement. It is an effort to which we hope we have contributed.

Introduction—To The Student

The most important thing for you to remember as you begin this course is that writers learn to write by writing. Nothing can substitute for simply practicing writing.

Because writers often worry that their work is not perfect, the hardest part of writing is getting started. During this course you will first simply think onto paper without regard for whether your ideas make sense or whether your sentences are properly written. The purpose of this kind of prewriting is for you to scribble down your thoughts and see where your writing may take you. After you have done plenty of mental exploring to discover what you think and how you feel, you will be able to choose a writing topic that is meaningful to YOU.

Once you discover a topic, you will have an opportunity to focus in on it and write about it a number of times, refining your thoughts as you go. All along the way your classmates and you will be discussing how your writing is going, giving each other feedback, reading aloud to each other, reacting as fellow writers and as potential readers. No doubt you and your classmates will go through at least a couple rough drafts until you are satisfied with the way you have expressed your ideas. Not until you are pretty well pleased with your paper should you worry about surface concerns such as punctuation.

To help you make your sentences look and sound the way you want them, you will learn to use some basic sentence forms. You will also practice various ways to add the details that help you get your ideas across. There will even be time to fuss with the fine points of writing when you edit your best pieces to submit in a portfolio for final evaluation.

Thoughtfully writing about things that are meaningful to you will help you develop the critical, reflective habit of mind that is essential to your college education. But there are no shortcuts. You can't do it overnight. It will take time to write, to get feedback, to rewrite, to think, to discuss, and to write again and again and again.

Acknowledgments

We extend our deepest thanks to the following:

Mary King—for starting us on this project in the first place, and for her thoughtful, encouraging comments throughout the process.

Basic Writing teachers at the University of Akron—the professionals who extensively class tested the sentence combining sections and who offered invaluable insight.

Basic Writing students—who submitted their work for this text and whose reactions helped us understand "what works."

Basic Writing peer tutors—who gave us yet another perspective on the project.

The many student writers of all levels with whom we have worked in the Writing Lab—Watching their writerly behavior helped us form our concept of what writers do and what kinds of things help novice writers become more expert.

Judy Knotts—special thanks for her editing checklist and for her enthusiasm for teaching.

The most interesting group of collaborators anyone could ask for, our reviewers—

Carol Aikman, Indiana University/Purdue University at Fort Wayne

Sandra Blakeman, Hood College

Patricia Burnes, University of Maine

Danny Cantrell, West Virginia State College

Patricia Eney, Miami University at Middletown

Eleanor Howes, Louisiana State University

Patsy Krech, The University of Memphis

Linda Lincoln, University of Minnesota

Deborah Murray, Kansas State University

Jen Navicky, Muskingum College

Vivian Sinou, Lake Tahoe Community College

Nancy Sorkin, Philadelphia College of Textiles and Science

Clark Baxter and Linda Poirier—who guided us through the sometimes murky world of writing a textbook.

We have enjoyed the journey.

Fluency

> *I* In the early stages of writing in this class you are encouraged to write as freely as possible, exploring your own experiences and feelings. The goal is to build fluency through self-discovery.

FREEWRITING

Freewriting is simply thinking onto paper, not worrying about what you say or how you say it, just writing down your thoughts. Freewritings sometimes even help you discover things about yourself that you may not have realized before. Although you may be surprised at what you write, you need not let it concern you that your new ideas are not yet fully developed, for freewritings are not finished pieces to be presented to the public. View them as a kind of thinking aloud that you do not need to share with anyone else.

If freewriting seems difficult at first, it is only because we naturally desire to reach closure in our writing rather than let ourselves explore or discover the many ideas that are swimming around in our heads. Even though you will not need to worry about grammar, punctuation, or spelling at this point, some discipline is required to simply avoid focusing on the first idea or topic that pops up.

To allow your mind time to work, you should move away from the temptation to write about something that you have already written about and force your thoughts into new directions, looking at a general topic from many angles, and taking little side trips in your mind.

The following freewriting drills or explorations can be used anytime that you feel blocked in your writing. You can use them in the classroom or on your own.

Three-Minute Drill #1

Write for three minutes without stopping. Write about anything that is on your mind. If you get stuck, jump to another topic, even if that topic is about how hard it is to write for three minutes!

Now look through your freewriting and choose one or two sentences (or maybe your entire three-minute exploration) to read aloud in class. As you listen to your fellow writers read aloud, use the opportunity to begin understanding the interests of your classmates.

Three-Minute Drill #2

The following pairs are set up as contrasting ideas that you can write about for three minutes each. Write about either side of a contrast—or about both sides, if you prefer.

Things I Love—Things I Hate

Things I Want—Things I Have

Things I Like About Myself—Things I Hate About Myself

How I Am Like Other Students—How I Am Different From Other Students

My College Hopes—My College Fears

Again, share selections from your pieces with the class, listening for interesting ideas and for viewpoints different from your own.

Nonfocus Drill—Five Minutes

Write for five minutes without stopping. Every time you find yourself wanting to go with an idea, run away from it. It's all right to write your reaction, "No, I won't write about my summer vacation!" Let your mind wander from topic to topic, mentally visiting memories or feelings and then moving on. You may be surprised where this exploration will take you.

After writing, share with your classmates as much of your exploration as you feel comfortable reading aloud. You will no doubt get to know each other better—and learn a few things in the process!

Freewriting on a Topic—Ten Minutes

Here is one student's ten-minute freewriting. Notice how the writer allows herself to jump from topic to topic without concern.

The neighborhood water fight I was one of the last to get wet. Tony Matos carried me up the stairs when I was hit in the eye with a softball. It knocked me out. He was so cute. Everyone liked him He was about 5 yrs older than me. Mo and Jo's friends. Fighting Cathy. Playing in the sand box at the Cales' and first learning how to swim. I'm going blank. Crap! Big crap okay In Canada where my aunt lives. Swimming in Lake Ontario. Catching Minos and Swimming under water for a long time Olympic Swimmer here! Trying out for cheerleading and making it. I screamed. Flunking forth grade. I hated those dam nuns! They were so mean. Especially Sister Ema. From old old Italy. Stricter than hell! Putting me in the trash can for talking. She needed to stand in the trash can. Matt & Mel pouring dirty old muddy flower & water on me and me scratching her face off. Don't mess with me boy. Back then, anyway. Loved playing dodge ball with Missy & Tim. All cousins. I was cool. I was the youngest. 4 yrs younger. I fell off a moped and put a hole in my knee. My mom yelled at me for getting on one.

I remember sitting in my room and thought we had rats in my closet When my cat had kittens. They were meowing and I thought sqeking I also remember moving away Crying so hard like have never cried before. I was leaving all of my friends, to a new environment. Ruthie &

Candance. Thats what I called Candace my new
friends we egged & teepeed. Played with Spiders.
Killing ants and putting them in spider webs.
Fun. Shawn My first crush. Jason my first
boyfriend. Both of them make we want to throw
up now. I'm done!

How many possible topics did you find in the above freewriting?

Discovering a Topic

At this point you have a number of freewritings, which you should consider exploratory pieces. Take a block of time to *read through all your explorations* and mark or underline ideas that seem interesting. You may see thoughts or concerns or possibly a few sentences that strike you.

Choose one sentence or idea, and write it at the top of a blank page. Now, once again, use your freewriting skills to explore this idea.

Beginning to Focus

Write for five minutes, sticking to the new idea. See where it will lead you.

You must be flexible! Don't worry if your hand takes you in a direction that you did not anticipate. You are *not* obligated to stick with your original thought. If you hit an absolute dead end, don't be afraid to return to your other explorations for another lead.

Getting Feedback

When you finally have a piece that is about something that interests you, get feedback from a group of fellow writers. Read the piece aloud. The members of your group should each write a brief response that includes:

I think the main thing you are trying to say is . . .
I was a little confused about . . .
What I would like to know more about is . . .

These initial responses should *not* be judgmental in any way. For now, the listeners should refrain from commenting on what they thought was good or weak about the piece. This is still a somewhat exploratory stage, and the feedback is to *help the writer make choices* rather than to tell the writer how to shape the piece.

Remember, this feedback comes from other students, and you are not obligated to follow their suggestions. However, all feedback is helpful because it gives you a sense of how others perceive your work. It may also lead you to think about your topic in new ways.

"Cutting a Slice" (Freewriting for Details)

At this point, your writing may have the quality of a list of ideas, events, or experiences. You may sense that you need to develop your ideas more fully to help your readers see what you see and feel what you feel.

Here is how one writer focused and expanded a small section of an exploration. The following piece about Sister Emma came from the earlier freewriting. If you look back, you will see the sentences:

```
I hated those dam nuns! They were so mean.
Especially Sister Ema. From old old Italy.
Stricter than hell! Putting me in the trash
can for talking. She needed to stand in the
trash can.
```

For this writer, that was enough to develop an entire piece of writing that tells a complete story. She found a focus by selecting one small incident from her freewriting. Here is how it worked out:

```
    I have many memories of my grade school years
at St. Anthony's. One of them is an experience
I had with may first grade teacher, Sr. Emma.
She was the strictest nun in the whole school.
She towered over the first graders, intimidated
us by forcefully pounding her index finger into
our chests while she scolded us with her
Listerine-coffee smelling breath. This is why I,
as well as the rest of my classmates, tried to
```

come to class prepared. If not, we would face that punishment along with standing in the trash can in the corner of the room, and we could not do that.

One rainy fall morning I was riding to school with my homework completed. After I kissed my mom goodbye I slammed the door, like I did every morning. As my mom started to drive away, I realized I slammed my bookbag in the door. I started running along side of the car, pounding on the window, screaming my moms name while tugging my bookbag to come loose from the door. But the car was going too fast so my body started dangling off the side of the car. Finally my bookbag came loose to make me fall in the middle of the street. As I was about to get run over by a van, the safety patrol man came and picked me up out of the street. My mom saw what happened in the rear view mirror and came running down the street in tears. The safety guy gave me to her.

My mom took me to First Aid with my scraped knees, muddy socks, and wet bookbag. My mom as well as Sr. Emma asked me why I didn't let go of the bookbag. I told her that my flashcards and homework were in it, and no matter what I was not going to let go because I did not want to get in trouble. Sr. Emma looked at me with a perplexed look and then said, "Get cleaned up. Let's go!" That damn nun had no remorse.

The memory is still very clear to me. I guess you would have to have been in my shoes, but nothing was going to stop me from leaving my

homework in that door and having to face the
wrath of Sr. Emma!

Now try taking just one event out of your piece. (We call this *cutting a slice.*) Put your reader "inside your head" and write as much as you can about the statement while staying focused on that particular moment. Include your personal reactions at the time. Now read your expanded "slice" aloud in your group and compare it with the original. What do you notice?

DRAFTING

Writing a Rough Draft

Now that you have found a tentative focus, something you really want to write about, it is time to start drafting, thinking in terms of a piece with a beginning, a middle, and an end. Start with a focused freewriting or a detailed "slice" to write up as a preliminary rough draft. You will need to do a number of rough drafts before you are ready to finalize a paper.

Even at this stage let your writing take you where it wants to go. Sometimes a sentence will appear at the end of a draft that really needs to go at the beginning. Don't be afraid to mess up your draft with arrows, numbers, and so on. Feel free to rearrange your draft and to write again.

In the drafting process you should try to build in as many reactions to events as you can. Use the margins and spaces between lines to add your own feelings, reactions, and examples, similar to the "cutting a slice" exercise.

Checking for Focus

After you have written your preliminary rough draft, read it through. If possible, read it aloud, pretending that you are hearing it for the first time. Ask yourself:

"What is the main thing I want someone to know?"

Write the answer to the above question on a separate piece of paper. Check your draft to see if the sentence appears anywhere. If it does, consider how well the draft sticks to this idea. If it does not, write another draft, using this idea as an opening sentence.

Getting Feedback

Now that you have a rough draft, it is time to read it aloud to your group to get the reactions of an audience.

1. First, tell your group members the point that you want your piece to make, and then ask them to listen for any specific concerns that you have. You may be worried about the piece's focus or about whether you got your point across. You may simply be concerned about whether the paper is interesting.
2. Then read the piece aloud to your group.
3. As you take turns listening attentively, help each other out by addressing the concerns that each writer voiced before reading. After those matters have been dealt with, listeners may feel free to ask about points that confused them and about items that they wanted to hear more about.

Important: The *writer,* of course, is the one who ultimately decides what stays, what goes, and what gets changed.

Using a Thesis Statement to Develop a Draft

So far you have written to discover feelings, thoughts, and ideas about your own experiences, developing and focusing them into fairly coherent pieces of writing. Now we turn our attention to developing a thesis. A thesis is a proposition or a claim that makes the meaning of the writing clear to the reader.

Remember the question for focus: What is the main thing I want someone to know?

Now you can ask the question: Why do I want someone to know it?

If you look back at the selection about the strict nun, Sister Emma, you can see some ideas in the text that are not directly stated. On the one hand, the narrator fears Sister Emma. But on the other hand, she may realize that she has learned something about the importance of following through on an assignment. What is the meaning of this experience? Is it that experience is sometimes a difficult teacher? That discipline is necessary in our lives?

When we decide how to state such an idea, we have begun to reflect on and analyze our experiences, explaining to others what our lives mean.

Exercise #1: In your group, see how many different thesis statements you can devise for the "slice" about the student who held onto the bookbag despite the danger. Then discuss how the writer would need to change or expand the slice to make it fit the different thesis statements.

Exercise #2:

1. Pick one of your drafts and write a practice thesis statement.
2. Read your draft aloud in a group and ask the other writers to write a statement about what the draft means to them.
3. Compare their statements with yours. You may be surprised at what they say, or you may hear something that you had not considered.
4. Select what you think is the best statement about the meaning of your paper, and write a draft that clearly reflects it.

A Focused Draft

As you read the following student draft, see if you can imagine how the writer followed the writing process that we have just practiced. There may be parts of this draft that you especially like, and there may be parts for which you have suggestions for improvement. Discuss your comments with your group.

```
        Why I Want to be a Child Psychologist


    I want to become a child psychologist because I
want to spend my life helping children who have
been abused. I have chosen this as a career,
for I have had to deal with sexual abuse myself
at the age of eleven by an uncle; therefore, I
can relate to these children. I remember the
tremendous fear I felt, for I knew what was
happening was wrong. I felt helpless and feared
other men would do this to me. I didn't like
what he was doing to me and felt very uncom-
fortable about it.
    I wanted it to stop, but I didn't know how. I
remember having a lot of nightmares that all
```

men, including my dad, wanted to do this to me. This completely horrified me, and I didn't know what to do. I wanted to tell my parents, but my Uncle John told me no one would believe me if I told and they would hate me for trying to cause trouble in the family. He also informed me that when Christina, his youngest daughter from this marriage, was my age he would do the same to her. Christina was six years old at this time, and I became frightened for her.

One night, after a year of this abuse, I was watching *The Wizard of Oz,* and Dorothy just entered the land of Oz; therefore, the screen became very colorful and my dad asked me if John was doing anything to me. At first I said no, but I suddenly got this sick feeling in the pit of my stomach. Then my dad said that John and I have been acting strangely for quite some time. With some relief, I said that John had been molesting me.

About four years later, Christina came to my house and told me that her dad was showing her porn flicks and showing her how to have sex. Of course, she actually said it in child-like terms. Naturally, I became very upset and all my past feelings came to me all at once, but I didn't know what to do. I began thinking about it and came to the conclusion that I had to tell someone; consequently, I called my friend Stephanie and I ended up talking with her step-father, who was a police officer. The very next day I was called to the office at school, unaware what would happen next. When I reached the office, I was pulled into a room where there was a social worker from Children's Services, a police officer, a tape recorder, and the guidance counselor. They came to talk to me about what John did to me as a child. Again, all the feelings from the past came flooding back, for they made me tell in full details what was done to me. I felt so dirty and was completely ashamed, but this would be well worth it to save Christina from having it happen to her. I didn't want her to have to live that way, and to make it worse, she would have had to face her offender everyday. After four long hours of this torture, I thought it was over. Leaving school that day, I felt better than I had in a long time. That night as I was leaving for church, I found the social worker in my living room talking to my parents. Feeling scared, I tried to run out to catch the bus, but it was no use. My parents and the social worker stopped me to tell me that John was arrested after hearing the tape I made earlier that day and admitting to everything I had said. They all told me how proud they were of me, and the final relief came over me.

Not long after that, fifteen other minors came forward and said that John had molested them also, including his eldest daughter from a previous marriage. About a year later, Stacey, his daughter came looking for me, to thank me for putting him away. You see, John not only molested her, but took her virginity away; therefore, she held a lot of anger in because of the ordeal he put her through. In the end it was well worth saving other girls from this guy. Who knows how many other girls he would have raped or molested.

As adults we must look out for the signs that are often expressed in children, such as the child may be withdrawn, may have inappropriate sexual behavior, and may feel a lot of guilt. There are, however, effects that could last a child's lifetime, such as low self esteem, mistrust, problems with intimate relationships, drug abuse, suicide, and sometimes turning into offenders themselves.

There are a few things we can do to stop child abuse; furthermore, we need to teach our children about abuse. Teach them they have the right to say no, that they can come to you with their problems and you will always believe them.

Someday I want to get tougher laws on child offenders. I think we should first castrate offenders, then put them in the electric chair, starting off with low electrical currents getting stronger til they die, making them suffer the rest of their lives the way children have to. Maybe child offenders would think about it before they abuse the child.

As you can see, I feel very strongly about child abuse. I know what it does to a child firsthand. Since I want to change my experience from a bad thing to something I've learned from, I have chosen a career to help others who have been through the same traumatizing experience.

> Children are so special, the greatest gift
> from God. They are a miracle. Why someone would
> want to hurt them, I'll never know.

ONE STUDENT'S WRITING PROCESS

Each writer is unique and finds his or her own way from the freewriting to the completed paper. The following freewriting and drafts are offered as an example of one student's entire writing process, completed about halfway through the term.

What you see on the paper does not tell the whole story, of course. You cannot see the discussions that the student had with his classmates and with his tutor, but you can imagine something of Dave's thought process as you consider why he might have made the changes that appear on the page.

Freewriting: Sporting Events

In his freewriting, Dave explores a number of possible topics—baseball, water skiing, and then a promising idea about teaching his wife to golf. At the very end he brings up racing, almost as an afterthought.

> Sporting Events Freewriting
> Some of the sports that I was involved in
> was baseball back when I was growing
> up, I played for about the ages of 7
> until I was 16. I did real well in
> this america's game being voted to the
> postage country allstars twice I also
> like water skiing at west brach reservoir
> with the nice water as smooth as
> glass and the choppy water and the
> spray off the boat hitting you in the
> face and the feel of the sail board
> digging into the water as the board
> tilts over and grabs the water and

your on one ski the power of the
boat the feel of you against the water
will it win and make me crash in
a terrible head over heel tumble as my
body crashes to the water and skips
across the lake like a stone because of
the speed I also like golf with the wife
it ended up being really enjoyable expecially
after me chilling out and taking the
time to teacher her to play the game
she loved it and I had to take her out
and buy her a set of clubs for her to
play after only taking her out to play
only twice. Years ago I tried to do this
with her but because of a inmature
outlook on life and this experiance
was a total failure not only has
I think I have matured a little and
have learned to appreciatte her and
life a little more. The fun we have
by the always new trials + tribulation
in every new round of golf is amazing
once other thing I did was to go racing
with some friends back in 1972 at a place
in youngstown at an old airport this
was lots of fun and last only on year.

Draft #1

For his first draft, Dave decided to explore the idea of drag racing. He makes a number of changes in wording, adding details for clarification. There are a number of things that he will keep throughout the writing process. He is content with the focus and development of the work. He decides on an opening that he will keep in subsequent drafts.

SMOKEM UP

The first time I ever participate in a drag race took place on a warm summer night in the later part of June in 1973 ~~The memories of~~ my very first drag race ~~still live in my mind today~~. From the preparation of the car to the smell of burning tires the excitement was awesome. Being a cocky young man of about 19 years ~~old~~ *yrs of age*, I was just like every one else. My car had to be the fastest thing on four wheels. The car was an extremely nice ride, and was a cherry red 1970 Boss 302 Mustang. It came from the factory with a 300 hp. V8, 4 speed transmission, and 650 holly carburetor ~~with~~ *and* the only option missing was wings. This car felt like it could almost fly. Some friends at work ~~took~~ *would take* their cars over to ~~Youngstown~~ *race track in Youngstown to* drag~~way to~~ race almost every Friday night They kept asking me Dave *when* are you going to ~~come~~ *go* racing with ~~all of us this~~ *us on a* Friday *night*? ~~One day~~ *One day I got tired of the constant badgering so had by all* I *finally* agreed and a great time was about to ~~begin~~. *little did I know* The track was about a 30 minute drive from Kent using the interstate. We all were ~~pumped to~~ *so excited* we left town early so they could show me the around the track, before the races would start and we would have to qualify. I was starting to get about as nervous as a teenager on his first date. *When we arrived,* To my surprise this track was also the municipal airport. I was told that during a race ~~if~~ *a* airplane had to land, the race would be delayed until the plane was safely out of the way. After a walk around the grounds to look things over it was time to get down to business and get ready to race. Back in the pits the first thing I had to do was to unbolt the mufflers from the headers. Then every car had to

undergo an inspection for safety and to see
which class the car would race in. After all
the poking and prodding by the inspector under
the hood, in the trunk, and at my tires, the
car was okayed to run and given its class
sticker. One of my friends cars was also in ~~the~~
same class so this meant that we could end up
running aginst one another. This would make ~~both~~ our
~~our days perfect~~ night a lot of fun if this were to happen, but
the officials are the ones who picks your com-
petator. *more detail organize Try to shorten Beginning*
The next step was the time trials. Here is
where the real fun begins, a quarter mile of
burning rubber, roaring engines, and nothing but
speed. I drove my shiny red mustang into what
they call the burnout area. Here is the area ~~to~~ that is used,
warm up the car tires so they grab the track
the best that they can. To do this you spin
your tires a few times. I revved the engine up
and the roar from the exhaust was mind boggling
and just then ~~you~~ I pop~~ped~~ the clutch. The tires ~~are~~ started
squealing and smoking, then quickly I shut it
down and thought wow what a rush. *my adreneline started to rush through my veins as I,* ~~You then~~ pulled
into the staging area, and up ~~to a~~ at the white line beside
what is called the christmas tree. This ~~is just~~ so called Christmas tree,
a pole between the two lanes with two vertical
rows of six lights each. The top row of lights
are red, the next four rows are yellow, and the
bottom row is green. You watch your row of
lights and when get the green you go like a bat
out of hell down the track. When I was setting
here next to ~~the~~ this car I was waiting to race, and
I nervously looked at my competator as
for the lights to start. My mind was ~~racing~~ started to

just as fast as my engine. The lights started
down, and the roar from both cars became deaf-
ing. My hands started to sweat, [my pulse was racing] every muscle in
my body became as tense as a piano string. I
don't even think my eyes blinked as I tried to
anticipate the changing of the lights red, yellow, yellow, yellow, yellow. My heart was pounding in my chest like a hammer striking an
anvil, then in a split second the light turned
green. My right foot smashed the gas petal to
the floor, [with a thud] as my left foot popped off the
clutch. The car jumped forward and drove my
whole body back into the [Rolling off the] seat as the tires ~~were~~ [as they were]
spinning, ~~smoking, and~~ trying to get a grip
upon the asphalt track. A quick glance at the
tachometer tells me I'm almost at the first
shifting point as it winds toward 7000 rpm.
Then as my right hand reaches for the shifter
the engine reaches 7000 rpm. In a split second,
bang, I power shift the car into second gear.
Instantly the tires lost their grip upon the
track. The car started to skid sideways towards
the other lane as if I where upon an icy road. [patch]
[I was tightly gripping the steering wheel as if to squeeze all the life out of it My knuckles were beginning to turn white as.] Fear was starting to tear at my mind. [Those minutes seemed to drag on forever,] as I was
trying to decide what to do as car was careen-
ing out of control toward the car racing beside
me. I jerked the wheel to the right and let up
on the gas. The car responded as the rear end
snapped back around and started straight down
the track as [again] the tires once again began to dig
into the asphalt. Relief flooded over me as if
I was standing out in a [cool] rain, but we were still
involved in a race. My foot again slammed the

gas petal against the firewall. The engine let
out a thunderous roar, as the car lurched for-
as 300 HP was unleashed again
ward down the track, and sent the tachometer *needle*
spinning toward that magic number. As I powered
the shifter into third gear the tires broke
loose again, but this time I was ready for any
suprises. Ajusting the gas did the trick and in
an instant the tires stopped spinning and I was
shifting into fourth gear. The finish line was
flashed
just ahead, and as I ~~crossed it a~~ sigh of
across it a smile lit up ~~my face and a~~
relief came out of me as the adrenaline slowly
drained from my body. As I slowed down at the
end of the track and drove back into the pits
it was time to do a quick check. First it was
my pants to see exactly how scared I was, then
dry and
a reality check. Well everything was still in
good order so, I waited to hear my time and
speed over the P.A, 17.04 at 82 mph, that wasn't
so bad considering. This is pretty neat, I
think I'm going to get back in line and give
this a another shot.

Draft #2

In the next draft, Dave has incorporated his revised opening, but he is
pretty well satisfied with the piece, especially the vivid description.
He has deleted the part about racing against a friend, perhaps to
tighten his focus. He now begins to decide on placement of paragraphs by reading aloud and thinking about the function of each piece
of information.

                    SMOKEM UP

                    participated
    The first time I ever ~~partisapated~~ in a drag
race it took place on a warm summer night in
1973. Being a cocky young man of about 19 years

old✗ I was just like every one else. My car had
to be the fastest thing on four wheels. I was
proud of my car and it was an extremely nice
ride. It was a bright cherry red 1970 Boss 302
Mustang. It came from the factory with a 300
hp. V8, 4 speed transmission, and 650 holly
carburetor and I thought the only option missing
was wings. This car felt like it could almost
fly. ¶Some friends at work would take their cars
over to Youngstown dragway to race almost ever
Friday night They kept asking me Dave when are
you going to come racing with us? I got tired
of the constant badgering so one day I agreed
and a great time was about to be had by all.
¶The track was about a 30 minute drive from Kent
using the interstate. We were all so excited we
left town early so we could look around the
track. We used some of this time to stroll thur
the pits and mingle among the other drivers and
cars before the start of qualifing and racqing.
Looking at all this racing equipment just took
my breath away. I was starting to get about as
nervous as a teenager on his first date. To my
surprise I was told this track was also the
municipal airport. They explained that during a
race if airplane had to land, the race would be
delayed until the plane was safely out of the
way. After ~~a~~ finishing the walk around the grounds to look at
things ~~over~~ it was time to get down to business
and get ready to race. ¶Back in the pits the
first thing I had to do was to unbolt the mufflers from the headers. Then ~~every~~ the car had to
undergo an inspection for safety and to see

which class the car would race in. After all
the poking and prodding by the inspector under
the hood, in the trunk, and at my tires. The
car was okayed to run and given its class
sticker. ¶The next step was the time trials.
Here is where the real fun begins, a quarter
mile of burning rubber, roaring engines, and
nothing but speed. I then drove my shiny red mustang
into what they call the burnout area. Here is
the area that is used to warm up the car tires
so they grab the track the best that they can.
To do this you spin your tires a few times.
When I sat here watching the other cars as I
awaited my turn every nerve on my body tingled
as the smell of melting rubber, spinning tires,
and thundering exhaust overwelmed all of my
senses. I revved my car's engine up and the
roar from the exhaust was mind boggling as it
just added to the other cars deep throated
songs. Then with a snap I just ~~then you~~ popped
the clutch. The tires started to squeal and
smoke, then quickly I shut it down and thought
wow what a rush. ¶My adrenalin started to ~~rush~~ pulse thur my
veins as I pulled into the staging area. You
see there awaiteing my arriveal was my competition, ~~competi-~~
~~tion~~ beside what is called the christmas tree.
This so called christmas tree is just a pole
between the two lanes with two vertical rows of
six lights each. The top row of lights are red,
the next four rows are yellow, and the bottom
row is green. You watch your row of lights and
when get the green you go like a bat out of
hell down the track. ¶When I was setting here
next to this car I was waiting to race, and for

the lights to start. I nervously looked my competitor
~~petator~~ as my mind started to race just as fast
as my engine. The lights started down, and the
roar from both cars became deafing. My hands
started to sweat, every muscle in my body
became as tense as a piano string. I don't even
think my eyes blinked as I tried to anticipate
the changing of the lights red, yellow, yellow,
yellow, yellow. My heart was pounding in my
chest like an hammer striking an anvil, than in
a split second the light turned green. My right
foot smashed the gas petal to the floor with a
thud, as my left foot popped off the clutch.
The car jumped forward and drove my whole body
back into the seat as the smoke started ~~was~~ rolling off
the tires as they were trying to get a grip
upon the asphalt track. A quick glance at the
tachometer told ~~tells~~ me I'm almost at the first
shifting point as it's red needle winds toward
7000 rpm. Then as my right hand reaches for the
shifter the engine reaches 7000 rpm. In a split
second, bang, I power shift the car into second
gear. Instantly the tires lost their grip upon
the track. The car started to skid sideways
towards the other lane as if I where upon an
icy road. I tightly gripped the wheel as if to squeeze
all the life from it. My knuckles on my hands
were beginning to turn white as fear was starting to tear at my mind. These moments seemed to
drag on forever as I was trying to decide what
to do as my car was careening out of control
toward the car racing beside me. I jerked the
wheel to the right and let up on the gas. The
car responded as the rear end snapped back

around and started straight down the track again as the tires once again began to dig into the asphalt. ¶Relief flooded over me as if I was standing out in a cool rain, but we were still involved in a race. My foot again slammed the gas petal against the firewall. The engine let out a thunderous roar as 300 h.p. was uleashed once again. The car lurched forward down the track, and sent the tachometer needle spinning toward that magic number. ¶As I powered the shifter into third gear the tires broke loose again, but this time I was ready for any suprises. Ajusting the gas did the trick and in an instant the tires stopped spinning and I was shifting into fourth gear. The finish line was just ahead, and as I flashed across it a smile lit up my face and a sigh of relief came out of me, as the adrenaline slowly drained from my body. ¶As I slowed down at the end of the track and drove back into the pits it was time to do a quick check. First it was my pants to see exactly how scared I was, then a reality check. Well everything was still dry and in good order, so I waited to hear my time and speed over the P.A, 17.04 at 82 mph, that wasn't so bad considering. This is pretty neat, I think I'm going to get back in line and give this a another shot.

Final Draft: The Race

You may notice that even this final draft is not yet perfect. This is Dave's *draft.* He can use it later for editing, when he can attend to spelling and correctness.

By the time Dave gets to a final draft, he has added a new title and incorporated his paragraphing decisions. He has also generally cleaned up spelling and punctuation, although there are still a number of errors.

Dave is a writer who seems to perform different tasks at different stages in his writing. Once he found a topic that he was happy with, his primary concerns were to help the reader easily follow his story and see what he saw and feel what he felt.

THE RACE

The first time I ever participated in a drag race it took place on a warm summer night in 1973. Being a cocky young man of about 19 years old, I was just like every one else. My car had to be the fastest thing on four wheels. I was proud of my car and it was an extremely nice ride. It was a bright cherry red 1970 Boss 302 Mustang. It came from the factory with a 300 hp. V8, 4 speed transmission, and 650 holly carbure-tor. I thought the only option missing was wings, and felt as if this car could almost fly.

Some friends at work would take their cars over to Youngstown dragway to race almost every Friday night They kept asking me Dave when are you going to come racing with us? I became tired of the constant badgering, so one day I agreed, and a great time was about to be had by all.

The track was about a 30 minute drive from Kent using the interstate. We were all so excited we left town early so we could look around the track. We used some of this time to stroll threw the pits, and mingle among the other drivers and cars before the start of

qualifying and racing. Looking at all this racing equipment just took my breath away. I was
starting to get about as nervous as a teenager
on his first date. To my surprise I was told
this track was also the municipal airport. They
explained that during a race if an airplane had
to land, the race would be delayed until the
plane was safely out of the way. After finishing the walk around the grounds to look things
over, it was time to get down to business and
get ready to race.

   Back in the pits the first thing I had to do
was to unbolt the mufflers from the headers.
Then the car had to undergo an inspection for
safety and to see which class the car would
race in. After all the poking and prodding by
the inspector under the hood, in the trunk, and
at my tires. The car was okayed to run and
given its class sticker. The next step was the
time trials. Here is where the real fun begins,
a quarter mile of burning rubber, roaring
engines, and nothing but speed.

   I drove my shiny red mustang into what they
call the burnout area. Here is the area that is
used to warm up the car tires so they grab the
track the best that they can. To do this you
spin your tires a few times. When I sat here
watching the other cars as I awaited my turn,
every nerve on my body tingled as the smell of
melting rubber, spinning tires, and thundering
exhaust overwhelmed all of my senses. I revved
my car's engine up and the roar from the
exhaust was mind boggling as it just added to

the other cars deep throated song. Then with a snap I just then you popped the clutch. The tires started to squeal and smoke, then quickly I shut it down and thought wow what a rush.

My adrenaline started to rush threw my veins as I pulled into the staging area. You see, there awaiting my arrival was my competition beside what is called the christmas tree. This so called christmas tree is just a pole between the two lanes with two vertical rows of six lights each. The top row of lights are red, the next four rows are yellow, and the bottom row is green. You watch your row of lights and when get the green you go like a bat out of hell down the track.

When I was setting here next to this car I was waiting to race, and for the lights to start. I nervously looked at my competitor as my mind started to race just as fast as my engine. The lights started down, and the roar from both cars became deafing. My hands started to sweat, every muscle in my body became as tense as a piano string. I don't even think my eyes blinked as I tried to anticipate the changing of the lights red, yellow, yellow, yellow, yellow. My heart was pounding in my chest like an hammer striking an anvil, than in a split second the light turned green. My right foot smashed the gas petal to the floor with a thud, as my left foot popped off the clutch. The car jumped forward and drove my whole body back into the seat as the smoke started rolling off the tires as they were trying to get a grip upon the asphalt track. A quick glance at the tachometer told me I'm almost at the first shifting point as it's red needle winds toward 7000 rpm. Then as my right hand reaches for the shifter the engine reaches 7000 rpm.

In a split second, bang, I power shift the car into second gear. Instantly the tires lost their grip upon the track. The car started to skid sideways towards the other lane as if I where upon an icy road. I tightly gripped the wheel as if to squeeze all the life from it. My knuckles on my hands were beginning to turn white as fear was starting to tear at my mind. These moments seemed to drag on forever as I was trying to decide what to do as my car was careening out of control toward the car racing beside me. I jerked the wheel to the right and let up on the gas. The car responded as the rear end snapped back around and started straight down the track again as the tires once again began to dig into the asphalt.

Relief flooded over me as if I was standing out in a cool rain, but we were still involved in a race. My foot again slammed the gas petal against the firewall. The engine let out a thunderous roar as 300 h.p. was unleashed once again. The car lurched forward down the track, and sent the tachometer needle spinning toward that magic number.

As I powered the shifter into third gear the tires broke loose again, but this time I was ready for any surprises. Adjusting the gas did the trick and in an instant the tires stopped

spinning and I was shifting into fourth gear.
The finish line was just ahead, and as I
flashed across it a smile lit up my face and a
sigh of relief came out of me as the adrenaline
slowly drained from my body.

As I slowed down at the end of the track and
drove back into the pits it was time to do a
quick check. First it was my pants to see
exactly how scared I was, then a reality check.
Well everything was still dry and in good
order, so I waited to hear my time and speed
over the P.A, 17.04 at 82 mph, that wasn't so
bad considering. This is pretty neat, I think
I'm going to get back in line and give this a
another shot.

Control

> *B*y now you have developed one or more drafts, and you have concentrated on exploration, focus, and drafting. Now it is time to consider tightening up your control as a writer. It is important to look at the sentences in your drafts and to have a set of techniques that help you make your sentences look and sound pleasing to a reader.
>
> Let's first consider the idea of sentence completeness and how to recognize the complete sentences in your text.

SENTENCE RECOGNITION AND COMPLETENESS

In everyday conversation, we do not always speak in complete sentences; however, the sentence is the basic unit in *writing*. A writer begins a sentence with a capital letter and may end it a number of ways—a period, an exclamation point, a question mark:

> I am a freshman this year.
> Am I a little nervous?
> You bet I am!

But capitalization and punctuation alone do not make a sentence. Sometimes we write a series of words that look like sentences, but they just don't sound like sentences.

For example, read the following words aloud:

> ***Working just to make ends meet.***

This statement is punctuated like a sentence, but it doesn't sound right to the ear. There seems to be some essential information missing.

Working just to make ends meet can be made into a complete sentence a number of ways:

- The writer could simply add a subject and verb:

  "I was working just to make ends meet." (I **is the subject.** *Was working* **is the verb.**)

- The writer could add a larger sentence unit:

  "Working just to make ends meet, I was unable to save any money."

Practice recognizing sentences: Here are some groups of words that are punctuated as sentences. Some are sentences and some are not. Identify which are sentences and which are not. Discuss your answers in a group and then with the whole class.

		Sentence	Not a Sentence
1.	I was excited about attending college.	☐	☐
2.	My brother smiled.	☐	☐
3.	When he heard how nervous I was.	☐	☐
4.	After my first week at the University.	☐	☐
5.	I felt more confident about my abilities.	☐	☐
6.	As a student.	☐	☐
7.	Chased by a bumblebee.	☐	☐
8.	I ran.	☐	☐
9.	She dressed up today.	☐	☐
10.	Hoping she would run into someone special.	☐	☐

As you discussed the above items, you may have decided that incomplete sentences often communicate quite adequately when they appear within the context of a conversation. In writing, however, readers expect and need all the sentences to be complete.

Practice writing complete sentences: The following incomplete sentences (also called fragments) contain information that might be quite understandable in the context of an ordinary conversation. In writing, however, they cannot stand alone as complete sentences.

Read each fragment aloud. Then add words or rearrange the words to make each fragment into a complete sentence.

1. Packed up my three kids and left behind what little household goods I had.

   _____

   _____

2. Worrying about not knowing anyone in the area.

   _____

   _____

3. What someone looks like after diving on a grenade to save his buddy's life.

   _____

   _____

4. As I wondered how we were going to pay for all the pumpkins.

   _____

   _____

5. While I was stuck in dreary Ohio in the snow, rain, and cold weather.

   _____

   _____

6. Shook their heads in disbelief as the other team scored.

   _____

   _____

7. The huge masses of people leaving the stadium.

   _____

   _____

8. White siding, wood shingles, a bay window, and a four-car garage.

_____

_____

9. Down the road, admiring the houses on my street.

_____

_____

10. Grasshoppers, bugs, and all kinds of little critters.

_____

_____

11. As ten trees came crashing to the ground.

_____

_____

12. The sight of thousands and thousands of gallons of water pounding the rocks below.

_____

_____

13. Gave me the feeling that I was able to walk on water.

_____

_____

14. Packing up coolers with lots of food and packing suitcases with lots of clothes.

_____

_____

```
15. Produced high flames that would emit a lot of
    heat and keep me warm.
```

_____

_____

Composing: Work alone, with a partner, or in a group to write out ten complete sentences.

Go back through your explorations and/or drafts to find complete sentences that you like. Copy them down as they are or change them any way you wish. Read them aloud to help you check that each is indeed a complete sentence.

Or you can choose phrases or fragments (incomplete sentences) that you can _turn into_ ten colorful, complete sentences.

Reading Aloud to Recognize Sentence Completeness in a Paragraph

Once you have written one or more rough drafts of a paper, you may be fairly satisfied that your writing presents your ideas clearly. However, before turning in a paper for a grade, ALWAYS go back over your work and make sure that each sentence within your writing is complete.

One of the most effective ways to check for sentence completeness is to read your work aloud. This can be a bit tricky, for you already know what it is you mean to say, and your mind may unconsciously complete fragments as you are reading through your work.

One way to help yourself isolate each sentence in your mind is to begin by reading aloud the LAST sentence in a passage. Ask yourself if that sentence alone would make sense to a reader. Then, if you find that the sentence is not complete, change the sentence in any way that you wish so that you end up with a complete sentence. Next, find the sentence that appears just before that one, and read it aloud, asking yourself whether someone else would understand that sentence all by itself. Proceed reading your paper backwards until you reach the first sentence.

Here is a short paragraph that your class can practice reading aloud backwards and forwards together:

```
I am in big trouble. There is an important
assignment due soon. I am not sure when the pro-
```

```
ject is due. Because I was late to class. And
missed out on the details. Can you help me out?
```

Practice recognizing sentences within a paragraph: The following student-written paragraphs have been altered so that they contain some complete sentences and some incomplete sentences. Work alone or with a partner as you follow these steps:

1. Read the paragraph aloud from the beginning to the end. Try to identify whether each sentence is complete or incomplete.
2. Read the paragraph backwards. Now try to identify whether each sentence is complete or incomplete. Was it easier to pick out the incomplete sentences when reading from the first sentence or when reading from the last sentence?
3. Rewrite the paragraph, making sure that each sentence is complete.

Practice Paragraph #1

```
In July of 1991 I left the state of
Mississippi. I resigned from my city job. Kissed
my family and friends good-bye. Packed up my
three kids and left behind what little household
goods I had. My life seemed like it wasn't
going anywhere. Working just to make ends meet.
So I headed north in hopes of building a better
life for the kids and myself. I moved to Akron,
Ohio. Which is a peaceful small town compared
to the state I had left. I had a girlfriend,
Crystal. Who was a student at the university
there. She invited me and my family to stay
with her.
```

Practice Paragraph #2

```
I called Emily early in the week. And asked her
to do something for the next weekend. She
sounded kind of happy. That I finally asked her
out. But in the back of my mind I had a feel-
ing. That she would be more comfortable if we
```

did something with her friends. I quickly called around town. To see what everyone was doing that weekend, but nothing was going on. Oh well, I guess I would stay with my original plan. And just do something romantic by ourselves. I had a whole week to decide what to do. Who knows? Maybe something would come up. Later in the week.

Practice Paragraph #3

As I fell asleep that night. I felt like that evening had been my very first date turned upside down. Just like my first date, I had wanted to make a lasting impression on her, but this time the only thing we really remembered was Doug and Sheri arguing. I also wanted it to be a romantic night. Between just the two of us, but it turned out to be an evening of silliness. With the four of us. Although the evening wasn't what I originally planned. I wouldn't change it for the world.

Composing: Look at one of your own drafts or explorations. Read it aloud backwards and mark with a pencil every sentence that does not sound right or that you think might not be complete. Revise your sentences and discuss your revisions with a partner or group.

USING DETAILS AND DESCRIPTION

USING A SERIES TO ADD DETAILS AND AVOID REPETITION

Writers often use a series of nouns, verbs, or descriptive elements to add information to sentences and to make them more interesting. Series are also useful in helping writers avoid ineffective repetition.

The underlined words in the following sentences are called a *series* of words. Read the sentences aloud:

1. *When I make pizza, I like to add <u>pepperoni, mushrooms, onions, peppers, and sausage.</u>* [Series of nouns]
2. *I have learned how to <u>mix, toss, and bake</u> perfect pizza dough.* [Series of verbs]
3. *Mr. Montoni's pizza is always <u>fresh, hot, and juicy.</u>* [Series of adjectives]
4. *Mr. Montoni prides himself in <u>using fresh ingredients, being generous with toppings, and serving piping-hot pizzas.</u>* [Series of phrases]
5. *Emil's also serves pizzas that are <u>freshly made, loaded with toppings, and bubbling with cheese.</u>* [Series of phrases]

Notice:

- The word *and* appears before the final item in the series.
- Commas separate the items in the series. The commas make the sentences easier to read. (It is also acceptable to omit the comma that appears before the *and*.)

Punctuating: Add commas to the series that appear in the following student-written sentences.

1. The Browns the Eagles and the Cowboys all won their games last weekend.
2. Yesterday I had fun swimming jogging and bicycling.
3. Gumbo has crabs shrimp and oysters in it.
4. It only took one moment before the scent of herbs sauce and homemade bread almost knocked me over.
5. My favorite food is Italian foods like pizza spaghetti chicken Parmesan meatball sandwiches etc.
6. For starters, hot dogs are tasteless bland and disgusting.

7. After our picnic is over, we sometimes go home eat again and go to the movies.

8. I have kidney beans chili sauce and my own little secrets I put in my chili to make it extra good.

Practice: Alone, with a partner, or in a group, combine each group of sentences into one complete sentence. Be sure that your final sentence includes a correctly punctuated series.

1. I was totally worn down.
   I was limp.
   I was skinny.
   I was discolored.

   _____

   _____

2. I was scared.
   I was unsure.
   I was dreading the moment my parents walked in.

   _____

   _____

3. Everyone was having a good time sitting around in a circle.
   Everyone was talking about the past.
   Everyone was enjoying the great feast that had been prepared.

   _____

   _____

4. When you look at Adora face-to-face, you see a full face.
   You see a rounded face.
   You see a copper-toned face.

   _____

   _____

5. She has short, stubby legs.
   She has small feet.
   She has a rather full figure.

   _____

   _____

6. Her hard work helps make her a successful
   employee.
   Her leadership helps make her a successful
   employee.
   Her determination helps make her a successful
   employee.

   _____

   _____

7. She loves meeting new people.
   She loves learning new skills.
   She loves being productive.

   _____

   _____

8. Alicia visits all the discount outlets.
   She visits thrift shops.
   She visits specialty stores.

   _____

   _____

9. LaMar is supportive.
   LaMar is understanding.
   LaMar is eager to help.

   _____

   _____

10. My car stalled at the red light.
    My car lost power at the stop sign.

```
My car ran out of gas as I pulled into the
driveway.
```

_____

_____

Keeping "Balance" in Your Series

To make your sentences clear and easy to read, remember to use similar structures when writing words in a pair or in a series. Notice how much easier it is to read aloud the "balanced" sentences below.

Not Balanced	**Balanced**
1. Pets depend on you to provide them with food, water, and they need shelter, too.	Pets depend on you to provide them with food, water, and shelter.
2. At this time of the year, the corn stalks are tall, brown, and they are dried out.	At this time of the year, the corn stalks are tall, brown, and dried out.
3. They start methodically touching, turning, and then they lift each pumpkin until they find the perfect one.	They start methodically touching, turning, and lifting each pumpkin until they find the perfect one.
4. I enjoy hunting, fishing, or I also spend time with loved ones.	I enjoy hunting, fishing, or spending time with loved ones.

Practice: The "unbalanced" part of each of the following sentences is underlined. Read each sentence aloud to help you hear the imbalance. On the line following each sentence, rewrite the unbalanced part so that it matches the rest of the sentence.

Example: The rally was inspiring, awakening, and <u>motivated you to the cause.</u>motivating

1. *The alternator belt came loose, broke, and <u>it fell</u> onto the highway as I was driving.* _____
2. *My new Webster's Dictionary is good for home, school, and <u>I use it at the office</u>.* _____
3. *I like all sports except golf, <u>hitting a ball around a tennis court</u>, and hockey.* _____

4. *The room was cold, so I closed the windows, turned up the heat, and* <u>*then I asked for a blanket*</u>. _____

5. *As I lost control of the car, it spun out,* <u>*I rolled it into the ditch*</u>, *and hit the tree.* _____

Composing: Freewrite for ten minutes about a few people that you know or about an event that you attended recently. Read your freewriting aloud or to yourself. Then use your imagination as you write ten sentences about the people and/or the event. Have fun as you expand your sentences by adding a series of words or phrases to describe what you did, saw, felt, or thought about the people or event.

Remember:

- Separate each item in the series from the others by using a comma.
- Include a comma before the *and* that introduces the last item in the series.
- Read aloud to help you determine whether all items in your series are balanced.

USING ADJECTIVES TO HELP THE READER SEE

As a writer, you will want to help your reader develop a mental image of what you are trying to express. With the aid of your imagination, you can create vivid descriptions by judiciously using adjectives.

Adjectives are commonly thought of as words that describe a person, place, or thing. They answer the questions Which? What kind? How many?

The adjectives in the following student-written sentences are underlined. Read the sentences aloud.

1. My _thick_ sociology book has _complex_ terminology and _lengthy_ chapters.
2. The _frustrated_ suspect cursed as the _police_ officers escorted him to the _squad_ car.
3. The _icy_ road conditions caused the _morning_ traffic to back up.
4. The _defending_ champions were losing the _championship_ game but made a _remarkable_ comeback during the _breathtaking_ fourth quarter.

The above sentences may sound pretty ordinary at first, but read them aloud again without the underlined words. Discuss with your class how some of the underlined adjectives seem almost necessary to the sense of the sentence whereas others contribute to sharpening a reader's mental image.

Practice: Work alone, with a partner, or in a group as you enliven the following sentences by adding adjectives. Choose from the adjectives listed under each sentence or add adjectives of your own.

1. The students studied hours for the class they were attending at the university. [Possible adjectives: diligent, five, economics, well-known]

   _____

   _____

2. During the night, the dog barked at the traffic passing in front of his house. [Possible adjectives: cold, nervous, noisy, new]

   _____

   _____

3. When the visitor walked through the student center, he noticed students sitting in the chairs under the stairway. [Possible adjectives: nervous, crowded, congenial, comfortable, open]

_____

_____

4. The children eagerly carry their pumpkins to the hay wagon as they anticipate the faces they will carve on them for the night to come. [Possible adjectives: excited, orange, crowded, frightening, festive]

_____

_____

5. Hundreds of Canada geese flock to the fields for a meal and a rest from their journey south. [Possible adjectives: honking, corn, well-deserved, brief, exhausting]

_____

_____

Composing: Make a short list of some people, places, or events that you have seen or attended recently. Now think about the _qualities_ of the sights, sounds, and smells associated with ONE person, place, or event. Brainstorm a long list of words that describe your chosen topic.

Next, share your list with your group; feel free to help each other expand your lists. Also, help each other check that your list has lots of adjectives.

Remember:

- Adjectives describe people, places, and things.
- Adjectives answer the questions Which? What kind? How many?

Now write a paragraph describing your chosen person, place, or event. For this exercise, concentrate on adding descriptive words (adjectives) before nouns. Underline the adjectives in your sentences.

USING TWO OR THREE ADJECTIVES IN A ROW

You may find that you sometimes want to describe a person or a thing by using two or three adjectives in a row. The adjectives in the following sentences are underlined. Read the sentences aloud.

1. *I like a <u>rich, brown</u> crust on fried chicken.*
2. *I like a <u>rich, crisp, brown</u> crust on fried chicken.*

In the two examples above, the adjectives <u>rich, crisp,</u> and <u>brown</u> appear *right before* the noun that they describe (<u>crust</u>). In sentences like these, use a comma to separate the adjectives when it might also make sense to use the word *and* instead of the comma.

As often happens, you will have occasions to make choices between two correct ways of writing something, based entirely on what sounds best to you. Read the following sentences aloud:

3. *I like <u>sweet, hot, and moist</u> muffins in the morning.*
4. *I like <u>sweet, hot, moist</u> muffins in the morning.*

Example 3 is a series of adjectives before the noun, and it is punctuated just like any other series. But you might choose to write your sentence like example 4, without commas. In cases like these, you decide which sentence best fits your intentions.

Practice: The following are student-written sentences that have had all the adjectives removed. Make the sentences more interesting by adding two or three descriptive words in a row before as many nouns as you can.

1. The students in the car drove by the stadium.

   _____

   _____

2. A road led to the horizon.

   _____

   _____

3. The woman wanted to meet a man.

_____

_____

4. His house was covered with ivy.

_____

_____

5. The student rearranged her dorm room last night.

_____

_____

6. The servers at the restaurant wore uniforms.

_____

_____

7. As the bench broke, the fans fell to the floor.

_____

_____

8. The homeless person wore a jacket.

_____

_____

9. I stared at the chalkboard during my class.

_____

_____

10. As you pull into the driveway, you see the barn on the left of the house.

_____

_____

Composing: Have fun adding more adjectives to the sentences that you wrote for the previous Composing exercise, or use your lists to inspire you to write a new descriptive paragraph. In either case, make a special effort to include two or three adjectives in a row, all of which appear *before* the noun that they describe.

USING ADVERBS TO HELP THE READER VISUALIZE THE ACTION

Writers use adverbs to help a reader better visualize the action being described.

Adverbs are commonly thought of as words that expand or limit action words (verbs) or descriptive words (adjectives or other adverbs). They answer the questions How? When? Where? or To What Extent? In English we may place adverbs anywhere in the sentence that best conveys the meaning the writer wants to get across to the reader.

The underlined descriptive words in the following sentences are adverbs. Read the sentences aloud.

1. I _really_ like thick, gooey, bubbling cheese on hot, spicy _pizza._
2. Emil _carefully_ places the condiments on his _enormously_ thick pizza.
3. _Carefully,_ Emil places the condiments on his _enormously_ thick pizza.

Notice:

• Many adverbs end with the letters -_ly._
• Adverbs can be placed almost anywhere in the sentence as long as they sound pleasing and make sense.
• Adverbs usually require no special punctuation.
• When an adverb is used as an introductory word, a comma is placed after it, as in example 3 above.

Practice: Work with a partner or in a group as you add adverbs to the following student-written sentences. Choose from the adverbs listed after each sentence, or add adverbs of your own.

    1. We arrived at our colored, orange and brown
       motel in beautiful Orlando. [Possible adverbs: finally,
       brightly]

    _____

    _____

    2. Ali checked in while I checked out the warm,
       crystal-clear pool. [Possible adverbs: wearily, eagerly, pleasantly]

_____

_____

3. Ali and I spent the first, glorious evening
   playing pool and scoping out the girls. [Possible
   adverbs: wisely, happily, quietly]

_____

_____

4. We met two sweet Southern girls and asked
   them to go to Disney World with us. [Possible adverbs:
   soon, remarkably, politely]

_____

_____

5. Ali and I spent the next two fantastic,
   unforgettable days enjoying ourselves. [Possible
   adverbs: thoroughly, immensely]

_____

_____

6. After making up ten creative sentences for
   writing class, I got writer's cramp. [Possible
   adverbs: cheerfully, very, finally}

_____

_____

7. One night, after being grounded, I sneaked
   out of the old house. [Possible adverbs: unfairly, desperately,
   extremely]

_____

_____

8. While being chased by the cat, the baby mouse
   ran behind the stove and squeaked. [Possible adverbs:
   playfully, quickly, loudly]

_____

_____

9. Mrs. Johnson lost her job after the irresponsible plant closed. [Possible adverbs: sadly, recently, environmentally, unexpectedly]

_____

_____

10. I sat in my uncomfortable chair, waiting for the long test to begin. [Possible adverbs: nervously, anxiously, unbearably]

_____

_____

11. The crisp, bitter air hit us in the face as we got out of the car. [Possible adverbs: suddenly, swiftly]

_____

_____

12. The howling wind blew us around as we tried to climb the steep, muddy hill. [Possible adverbs: rudely, courageously, unbelievably]

_____

_____

13. We stood in line as the cold, powerful wind continued to blow. [Possible adverbs: anxiously, relentlessly]

_____

_____

14. As we exited the haunted house, we passed under a gray headstone. [Possible adverbs: timidly, carefully]

_____

_____

15. We talked as we walked down the slippery hill
    in search of the car. **[Possible adverbs: loudly, slowly]**

_____

_____

Adding adverbs to help a reader visualize the action: See how many appropriate adverbs you and a partner can add to the following student-written story.

Remember:

- Adverbs expand, describe, or limit action words (verbs) or other descriptive words (adjectives or adverbs). They tell How? When? Where? or To What Extent?
- Adverbs often end with the letters -*ly*.
- Adverbs can appear anywhere in the sentence, usually requiring no special punctuation.
- When an adverb is used as an introductory word at the beginning of a sentence, a comma is placed after it.

An Unusual Stranger

Black, cloudy night-time hung over the backdrop of the house. The grey, ramshackle walls of the house looked worn and forbidding, and the dilapidated stairway said to leave and not return.

The creaking floor met my feet with clouds of hanging dust as musty smells attempted to overcome me. The house's burned timbers watched me with growing malice. Darkened rooms made seeing impossible, and rotted woodwork broke at the merest touch. Scurrying rats made frightened sounds as I walked past. The collapsed roof moaned under the pressure of a cold, persistent wind, and black stagnant water filled the basement in an uninviting pool.

I saw the form of a girl hovering in the corner of a room. The floating form stood as the
most peaceful thing in the house. She moved
about the room and appeared to search for
things long since gone. She looked upon me as
the eerie wind howled between the timbers. She
faded and was gone. I wondered who she was, and
I wonder to this day.

Read your completed version of the story aloud to the class or to
another group. Notice how adverbs help the reader "feel" what is
happening as well as visualize it. What else did you notice about this
exercise?

Composing: As a class, in your group, or with a partner, brainstorm a
list of relatively ordinary events in your life. As a group or individually, draft a simple paragraph that tells *what happened* or *what happens*
during one of those events, step by step. Then go back and see how
many adverbs you can add to the sentences. Read your paragraph
aloud. How does it sound to you?

USING PREPOSITIONAL PHRASES TO SHOW RELATIONSHIPS

You probably use prepositional phrases regularly in your writing to show the relationship between certain details or ideas. Like adjectives and adverbs, they add description and details. The underlined phrases in the following student-written sentences are prepositional phrases. Read the sentences aloud.

1. I found twenty-five cents _on the ground,_ but I did not report the extra income _to the Internal Revenue Service._
2. Since I did not include the extra income _on my tax form,_ the IRS prosecuted me _for fraud._
3. I spent some time _in a federal penitentiary_ serving a twenty- to thirty-year sentence _for tax evasion._
4. I shared a cell _with a clown_ who was _in jail_ for jaywalking _during the middle of the night on a lonely country road._
5. _After a long drought in the middle of winter,_ the clown and I escaped _from prison on a flying carpet._

Notice:

*   Prepositional phrases can appear any place within a sentence.
*   Prepositional phrases require no special punctuation unless they begin a sentence. Then they may be separated from the rest of the sentence by a comma.
*   Prepositional phrases begin with words called prepositions.
*   Prepositional phrases end with a noun (or with a pronoun).

Here are some common prepositions:

about	at	by	inside	onto	until
above	before	down	into	over	up
across	behind	during	like	since	upon
after	below	except	near	through	with
against	beneath	for	of	to	within
among	beside	from	off	toward	without
around	between	in	on	under	

Practice manipulating prepositional phrases: Alone, with a partner, or in a group, rewrite the following student-written sentences. As you rewrite them, move some or all of the underlined prepositional phrases to a different position within each sentence. Remember to place a comma after prepositional phrases that begin sentences.

1. <u>Under the water</u>, my scuba gear malfunctioned.

   _____

   _____

2. The defending champions were losing <u>at the beginning of the game</u>, but they made a comeback <u>during the fourth quarter</u>.

   _____

   _____

3. I served <u>in the Persian Gulf</u> <u>during Operation Desert Shield/Storm</u>.

   _____

   _____

4. The average height <u>of men</u> <u>during the Middle Ages</u> was 5 feet 6 inches.

   _____

   _____

5. <u>Behind the shelf</u> <u>in the store room</u>, the small mouse was caught <u>in the trap</u>.

   _____

   _____

6. Everything was bright and alive <u>in the forest around me</u>.

   _____

   _____

7. <u>After a while</u>, I grew tired of walking and sat down <u>on a fallen tree</u>.

_____

_____

8. Suddenly, there was a movement <u>in the leaves off to the right</u>.

_____

_____

9. I sat <u>on the log</u> <u>for a long time</u>, watching life go on, just enjoying the woods.

_____

_____

10. I reached the edge <u>of the woods</u> before long and continued <u>through the meadow to my house</u>.

_____

_____

Practice using prepositional phrases to add details: Work alone, with a partner, or in a group as you add prepositional phrases and other words or phrases to the following sentences. Have fun creating interesting, perhaps humorous, sentences. Underline your prepositional phrases.

Here is the list of common prepositions from the beginning of the lesson:

about	at	by	inside	onto	until
above	before	down	into	over	up
across	behind	during	like	since	upon
after	below	except	near	through	with
against	beneath	for	of	to	within
among	beside	from	off	toward	without
around	between	in	on	under	

1. The mouse was caught.

_____

_____

2. The dog barked.

   _____

   _____

3. Maurice ate fried chicken.

   _____

   _____

4. Geraldo was shocked.

   _____

   _____

5. Children learn rapidly.

   _____

   _____

6. I took a walk.

   _____

   _____

7. Rob rested awhile.

   _____

   _____

8. We climbed the hill.

   _____

   _____

9. The children walked.

   _____

   _____

10. I am a first-year student.

_____

_____

Thinking / revising/ composing: Use the paragraphs you wrote for practice with adjectives or adverbs, or choose another paragraph from an exploration or draft that you have written. You may find that you already have a number of prepositional phrases within your paragraph. Underline the prepositional phrases.

Adjectives, adverbs, and descriptive elements of various kinds are some of the tools that a writer uses to create an image in a reader's mind. Think about the effect that you want to create as you revise your chosen paragraph, perhaps adding prepositional phrases, adjectives, or adverbs judiciously.

After you rewrite your paragraph, discuss it with your classmates, especially regarding the kinds of *choices* you made as you revised it. Discuss together the effect that the revisions have on those to whom you read it.

COMBINING SENTENCES

A writer can manipulate sentences in a number of ways to make them easier for a reader to read. Combining sentences is one way to do this. In this section you will have the opportunity to combine sentences by using coordination (giving the original sentences "equal" emphasis) and subordination (emphasizing one or the other original sentence).

USING COORDINATING CONJUNCTIONS TO JOIN COMPLETE SENTENCES

All the sentences in this paragraph are complete. Read the paragraph aloud.

```
My older brother Jon and I used to play neigh-
borhood football. He turned sixteen. He started
to drive. I was left at home alone. I played
with the neighborhood kids. It was not the same
as when Jon was there to play with us. The
other kids started getting their licenses. The
football teams started getting smaller. I could
hardly wait until I was old enough to drive. I
wanted to go out with Jon and the older guys.
```

Discuss with your classmates how you might make this paragraph easier to read by combining sentences to eliminate some of the "choppiness." (Remember: There is no one "right" way to do this.)

One of the most basic ways writers avoid choppy writing is by connecting two sentences with a comma and a coordinating conjunction. Here are some conjunctions that can be used this way:

,*and*—shows a simple connection between sentences

,*or*—shows a choice between sentences

,*for*—connects sentences only when it means *because*

,*but*—shows a contrast between sentences

,*so*—connects sentences only when it means *as a result*

,*yet*—means *but*

Read the following student-written sentences aloud. Discuss how the underlined conjunctions show a connection between sentences. Also think about other effective ways to connect the sentences.

1. *The woman jumped off the tall building, <u>and</u> everyone below screamed.*
2. *I would help you, <u>but</u> I don't know what the problem is.*
3. *He should stop feeling sorry for himself, <u>or</u> he will have even fewer friends.*
4. *I got tired of watching the movie, <u>so</u> I got up and drove to my girlfriend's house.*
5. *I asked Amber to help me, <u>for</u> she was also taking the class.*
6. *I am very tired from working, <u>yet</u> I still have homework to do.*

Practice: Alone, with a partner, or in a group, see how many effective ways you can use a comma and a coordinating conjunction to combine each pair of sentences.

1. Sometimes customers used foul language.
    I would go home with a headache.

    _____

    _____

2. The sun beat down on us.
    My dad warned us to put some lotion on before
    we got sun burned.

    _____

    _____

3. Writing hurts my hand after a while.
    I get a neck cramp from tilting my head.

    _____

    _____

4. Chris is someone I grew up with.
    My better judgment has prevented a friendship
    from occurring between us.

    _____

    _____

5. Did that actually happen?
    Was he lying once again?

_____

_____

6. Antonio has taught me how to do math.
   He knows what he is doing.

   _____

   _____

7. The new cars went up in price by eight
   percent.
   With all the incentives, the price averaged
   out to be the same as last year.

   _____

   _____

8. The engine sounded like an Indy car.
   It took off like a rocket.

   _____

   _____

9. I got this sinking feeling in my stomach.
   My throat became too dry to talk.

   _____

   _____

10. We had been through many combat training
    exercises.
    This was to be the real thing.

    _____

    _____

11. I am hungry.
    I have homework to do before I can eat.

_____

_____

12. The sky is a cornflower blue now.
    The rain will be here by this afternoon.

_____

_____

13. It was an interesting class.
    It had a lot of homework.

_____

_____

14. College is so much different from high
    school.
    I now am completely responsible for my actions.

_____

_____

15. I enjoy talking to my other friends.
    My girlfriend gets upset when I do.

_____

_____

16. I had a lot of dirty laundry.
    I spent the evening at the laundromat.

_____

_____

17. We came home early last night.
    We had a lot of homework to finish.

_____

_____

18. She wanted to pass her math test.
    She visited a tutor and studied hard.

    _____

    _____

19. I received a ticket on my windshield.
    I parked in the wrong parking lot.

    _____

    _____

20. I ran out of gas on the way to campus today.
    I forgot that my fuel gage was not working.

    _____

    _____

Composing: Jot down a list of words or phrases to remind you of the events of the past or the upcoming week. Use your list to create ten sentences that are a combination of two *complete* sentences, following the pattern that you have just practiced. To connect your sentences, choose from the conjunctions at the beginning of this lesson.

Remember:

- Connect the two sentences with the conjunction that best conveys the relationship you wish to create.
- Include the comma before the conjunction.
- Use each conjunction no more than twice.
- Read your sentences aloud to make sure that you have connected two *complete* sentences.

Possible exploration: Look through the sentences you wrote for the composing exercise or go back to the list you jotted down to get you started. Freely write about your feelings regarding one (or more) of the recent or upcoming events in your life. Include details to help you explain your feelings. Discuss your exploration with a partner or with your group. Might this exploration suggest a workable topic for a future paper?

USING COORDINATING CONJUNCTIONS TO JOIN PARTS OF SENTENCES

In your writing, you most likely already use *and*, *or*, and *but* to connect words and phrases that are not complete sentences. For example, read aloud the following:

1a. *College students can discover ways to balance their studies.*
     College students can discover ways to balance their social lives.

These sentences can be connected to read:

1b. *College students can discover ways to balance their studies <u>and</u> their social lives.*

2a. *I can sign up for math tutoring on Mondays.*
     I can sign up for math tutoring on Tuesdays.

These sentences can be connected to read:

2b. *I can sign up for math tutoring on Mondays <u>or</u> Tuesdays.*

Notice: When you connect *parts* of two sentences by using a coordinating conjunction, *do not* use a comma before the conjunction.

Practice: Alone, with a partner, or in a group, combine parts of the following student-written sentences to create one complete sentence.

1. I feel that writing is a good way to express one's feelings.
    I feel that writing is a good way to express one's thoughts.

    _____

    _____

2. Freewriting brings my feelings out into the open.
    Freewriting relieves stress.

    _____

    _____

3. I enjoy writing about my family.

I enjoy writing about my friends.

_____

_____

4. My classmates hate to write just to fill
   time.
   I hate to write just to fill time.

_____

_____

5. After spending time collecting information,
   I'm ready to combine it all.
   I am ready to create a masterpiece.

_____

_____

6. When I get tired, I normally have to take a
   break.
   I return later with a positive attitude.

_____

_____

7. If it weren't so noisy, I could hear the
   professor.
   If it weren't so noisy, I could concentrate
   on the lecture.

_____

_____

8. Writing papers makes my hand hurt.
   Writing papers sometimes gives me a headache.

_____

_____

9. I didn't think college would be so hard.
   I didn't think college would require so much study time.

   _____

   _____

10. My kids are having a hard time calming down after the long, exciting day.
    I am having a hard time calming down.

    _____

    _____

11. My daughter wants to be a cheerleader.
    She wants to be a ballerina.

    _____

    _____

12. Valerie has a lot of pride in her work.
    Angela has a lot of pride in her work.

    _____

    _____

13. My coworkers had a great time remembering our baseball game against a rival firm.
    I had a great time remembering our baseball game against a rival firm.

    _____

    _____

14. My friend Antonio is self-assured.
    He is unreliable.

    _____

    _____

```
15. University Orientation class helped me
    organize my time.
    University Orientation class helped me
    organize my money.
```

_____

_____

Composing: Write ten creative sentences of your own in which you connect _parts_ of sentences without using a comma. You might want to proceed as follows:

- Make a list of people or events that are part of your weekday (or weekend) routine(s).

- Use coordinating conjunctions _without commas_ to connect pairs of people, events, actions, and/or characteristics as you write sentences about them.

Possible exploration: Go back to one of your recent explorations. "Cut a slice" from it and freely write in detail, either about your feelings or about physical details and actions. Share your slices with a partner or a group and discuss how well they enabled your readers or listeners to see what you saw and feel what you felt.

USING COORDINATING CONJUNCTIONS WITHIN A PARAGRAPH

You have just completed lessons about joining complete sentences with a coordinating conjunction preceded by a comma (to signal that a new sentence is coming up after the conjunction) and about joining *parts* of sentences with a coordinating conjunction and *no* comma.

It takes a bit of concentration for a writer to get the comma right every time. Here is a student-written draft for you to practice making the necessary distinctions between complete sentences and parts of sentences.

Practice recognizing complete sentences and parts of sentences: The student who wrote the following draft correctly used a number of coordinating conjunctions. As you read the story aloud, mark all the coordinating conjunctions that you find. Then discuss with your group why some of the conjunctions have commas before them and others do not.

Crash! The stock boy muttered an oath as several glass jars broke in the aisle. After he noticed I was there, he turned beet red and quietly went about his business of cleaning up the mess.

"Mom, did you hear that? I would never swear like that," I laughingly whispered at the age of sixteen.

"Mom?" Hearing no quick retort to my comment, I turned around only to see an empty aisle. Waiting for what seemed like a few minutes but was only a second, I saw a cart turn the corner, but instead of my mom, it was some old lady coming towards me. She started asking me for help in reading a label and asked me what brand of soup she should choose. I answered as quickly as possible and made a mental note that even my mom wasn't that old! Then I said, "Excuse me. I have to find my mom!" I started to jog down the aisle, skirted around the stock boy and was sure I would run into my mom just around the corner.

Where the heck could she be!

I thought if I stayed in one place and listened for her voice I would be sure to find her. Actually, all I heard was elevator music, some kid crying for Pop Tarts with frosting, another mother telling her son to stop ramming the cart into the back of her legs, and that old lady still trying to figure out what brand to buy.

Bread. I know she said we needed bread. Now which way is that department? Pickles. Baking supplies. Frozen foods. Pet food. Paper products. Finally, the bakery. Still no mom!

"Good grief! Where is that woman? Why does she decide to lose me when I'm in a hurry to get home?" I can't believe I'm standing here talking out loud to myself. Here comes that old lady again, asking if I like Italian or rye bread.

As I'm starting to get frustrated, I remind myself that I'm an adult. I should certainly be able to find my mother in a grocery store. I start the search from the now empty bakery.

I begin to notice that the store is filling up with people stopping in after work for a few items—moms and dads with small kids hanging all over them after a day with the sitter, but I still don't see my mom. There are many moms and dads dressed for success, but I still don't see my mom. Some moms look like aerobics instructors, but that's another story.

Think, Mark, think, where could the woman who only a few years ago wouldn't let you cross the street alone have gone to? If she thinks that this is some sort of joke to make me late setting up plans for the evening, she has another thing coming! When I find her, I'm going to let her know just how ticked off I really am. This is no joke!

Again the old lady, this time asking the price per ounce of Downy. I want to say, "Look, lady, get a life!" Instead, I answer her question politely and take off running before she comes up with something else.

Now I must look like a fool because the lady behind the deli counter asks if she can help me find something, "Yeah, my mom!" She laughs and then starts to help the old lady, who is now asking what type of ham is the best, low salt, honey baked, or Bavarian. Please God, let me get away from that woman for more than a few minutes!

"Enough of this," I tell myself. "Just go to the doors at the front of the store. See if she is checking out. If she isn't in line, maybe she is already by the car waiting for me." Still no mom!

Oh, no! That old lady is counting the items to see if she can get into the express lane. Someone help me before I take her and her groceries and send them flying through those stupid automatic doors.

Just as I'm ready to scream, I feel a tap on my shoulder. There is my mom, handing me one of those helium balloons that says, "I think you are terrific." She takes one look at me and realizes that I am not pleased with her or the balloon. Her smile turns into a look of rejection and hurt, and all I can think of is how pissed off I am because of the time I wasted going to the store "just to pick up a few things."

To make matters worse, here comes that old lady with her bag of groceries, asking what is best for the environment, plastic or paper. Does the world care, lady? Does the world really care if you use paper or plastic? Just shut up already and get out of my way!

I think I'm about to explode from frustration when the old girl turns to my mom and says, "What a handsome young man. You must be very proud of him. He was a help to me while I was shopping. My family isn't close by and my sight isn't what it used to be. It was nice talking to him while I was shopping."

Shocked by her words, I stop, look at my mom and think, "Please God, when she is old and shopping alone, please, please, let there be some kid there who is separated from his mom."

Composing: Use a draft of your own to practice using coordinating conjunctions in a number of ways:

1. Read through the draft and mark all the coordinating conjunctions that you find in it.
   - Be sure that there is a comma before the conjunctions that separate complete sentences.
   - Conjunctions that do not separate complete sentences do not require a comma before them—unless they are part of a series.
2. Reread your draft aloud and mark those sentences that might sound more effective if they were combined with a coordinating conjunction, either by combining complete sentences or by combining parts of sentences.

- Rewrite the sentences you chose, and then read your revised version of your draft aloud.

Possible exploration: Alone, jot down your feelings about your development as a writer thus far this semester. You may wish to include your assessment of your writing as you began the semester, what you had expected to learn, what you have learned so far, and what you hope to accomplish by the end of the term. You may also want to include how you plan to reach your goal.

You can think of this exploration as a personal diary entry, recording your growth as a writer. On the other hand, the exploration might lead to an important discussion about which you may wish to write more.

USING SEMICOLONS TO JOIN COMPLETE SENTENCES

Occasionally you may want to connect two sentences without using a conjunction. For the most part, any two sentences that have a clear relationship and can logically be written one right after the other can be connected with a mark of punctuation called a semicolon. Here are some sentences connected with a semicolon. Notice that the second sentence explains, comments on, or gives details about the first sentence.

1. I want to improve my writing ability; I am taking Basic Writing to refresh my skills.
2. College Reading helps students improve their vocabulary skills; it also teaches them how to read their textbooks more effectively.
3. Sometimes I can focus my freewriting easily; on other occasions I change my mind several times before deciding on a focus.
4. I usually handwrite my rough draft; once in a while I type it up on a PC in the computer lab.
5. The students in my class want to help each other with their papers; we do our best to listen carefully as we take turns reading aloud.

Notice:

- There is a complete sentence on each side of the semicolon.
- The relationship between the sentences is relatively clear to a reader.
- The word that appears after the semicolon is not capitalized.

Punctuating: The following student-written sentences may be punctuated by using a semicolon between complete sentences. Insert a semicolon in the proper position.

1. He plays the drums very well he is sure to be successful when he plays with the band.
2. Studying for my test seemed to take forever I stayed up until midnight.
3. I have no idea what to do my speech on I have to decide on my topic by Wednesday.
4. I hate my present job I need to make money somehow.
5. Today is my birthday I am going fishing.

6. Tom robbed a bank and shot a man he has a long prison term to serve.

7. I am returning to school after ten years I have to work harder to keep my grades up.

8. The policeman wrote me a ticket for speeding he also had a warrant for my arrest.

9. The officer was going to write Dave a ticket Dave is a smooth talker and got out of it.

10. Greg was running after Kathy he could not catch her.

Composing: Go back to the sentences that you composed for the lesson on joining complete sentences. Rewrite five of your completed sentences, connecting the parts with a semicolon.

• You may need to reword the sentences to make their relationship clear.

• Read aloud to help yourself hear whether you have a complete sentence on each side of the semicolon.

• Discuss with your group whether the sentences sound better when the parts are joined with a semicolon or with a comma followed by a coordinating conjunction.

Possible exploration: Think back to your earliest reading or writing experiences. You may wish to go all the way back to your preschool experiences or to more recent years. Brainstorm a list of your memories with reading or writing. Perhaps include stories that were read to you or that you read yourself, either voluntarily or as an assignment. This may be an exploration that you will want to focus more and more tightly until you rediscover a significant literacy experience in your life.

USING A SEMICOLON AND A TRANSITIONAL WORD TO JOIN COMPLETE SENTENCES

Joining two sentences with only a semicolon requires the reader to figure out the relationship between the two sentences. Most of the time, a writer wants to make things easier on the reader and simply *tells* the reader the relationship between the two sentences.

Here are some common transitional words and phrases that can be used after a semicolon to connect two sentences. When they are used this way, they are followed by commas.

; therefore		
; thus	} means *as a result*	
;consequently		
;then	} show a time	
;finally	relationship	

;however		
;nevertheless	} mean *but*	
;furthermore	} means *and*	

The following are sentences from the previous lesson. They have been connected with a semicolon *and* a transitional word.

1. I want to improve my writing ability; *therefore,* I am taking Basic Writing.
2. College Reading helps students improve their vocabulary skills; *furthermore,* it teaches them how to read their textbooks more effectively.
3. Sometimes I can focus my freewriting easily; *however,* on other occasions I change my mind several times before deciding on a focus.
4. I usually handwrite my rough draft; *nevertheless,* once in a while I type it up on a PC in the computer lab.

Notice:

- There is a complete sentence on each side of the semicolon.
- The semicolon is placed at the end of the first sentence.
- The transitional word begins the second sentence.
- A comma is used after the transitional word.

Punctuating: The following sentences have been correctly connected with a transitional word. Add a semicolon where the first sentence ends. Add a comma after the transitional word that begins the second sentence.

1. It is hard for me to get started writing therefore I use freewriting to get my thoughts flowing.

2. First I get my scattered thoughts down on paper then I decide which idea is the one I want to focus on.

3. I organize the thoughts in my focused freewriting by numbering sentences and drawing arrows all over my paper consequently my rough draft is fairly easy to write.

4. Fellow students often have helpful suggestions nevertheless each writer must take responsibility for his or her own paper.

5. Proofreading is an important step in the writing process however it is the *last* step.

Practice: Combine each pair of student-written sentences by using a semicolon followed by an appropriate transitional word and a comma. Work alone, with a partner, or in a group.

1. I have been reading in the dim light all evening.
    My eyes are becoming bloodshot.

    _____

    _____

2. Maurice was injured in an accident at work.
    He won't be coming to your party.

    _____

    _____

3. Sarah was eager to cook a large meal.
    She decided to go out for a light snack.

    _____

    _____

4. I planned to wash the car today.
    The weather is way too cold.

    _____

    _____

5. I need money for the rent and truck payments.

This month's college tuition is due by the fifth.

_____

_____

6. I want to fit too much information into a sentence.
   Sentences sometimes seem to go on and on for me.

   _____

   _____

7. My father was sent to Vietnam.
   Some twenty years later, I was sent to the Persian Gulf.

   _____

   _____

8. I need to finish my algebra by Tuesday.
   My science assignment is also due that morning.

   _____

   _____

9. The speed limit was raised to sixty-five.
   People still continue to speed.

   _____

   _____

10. The manager was not hiring anyone at the time.
    He encouraged me to fill out an application.

    _____

    _____

11. I have trouble speaking French.
    It is required for my major.

    _____

    _____

12. I am new at using a word processor.
    Right now it would be easier to handwrite my
    paper.

    _____

    _____

13. I ran the red light.
    The officer pulled me over.

    _____

    _____

14. I lost my job today.
    The bank is foreclosing on my house.

    _____

    _____

15. Our toddler was running down the street.
    We were able to catch him before he got hurt.

    _____

    _____

Composing: Take a few minutes to pick out some sentences that you have composed yourself. You might want to work with the sentences that you connected with coordinating conjunctions or with the sentences that you connected with a semicolon.

Using a semicolon and an appropriate transitional word, connect some of your sentences so that you have a total of ten completed sentences.

Remember:

- Choose a transitional word that best conveys the relationship between the two sentences.
- Use appropriate capitalization and punctuation.
- Read aloud to make sure that you have a complete sentence on each side of the semicolon.

Possible exploration: Look back at some earlier examples of your writing, and underline transitional words. Try adding new transitional words to make the relationships in the writing clearer. Read the revised piece aloud. Which one seems more effective?

USING DEPENDENT/SUBORDINATE CLAUSES TO SHOW RELATIONSHIPS BETWEEN IDEAS

Read the following groups of words aloud:

1. *Because college students deserve help with their writing*
2. *Whenever you have writer's block*
3. *If you consult with a tutor regularly*

Your knowledge of the English language allows you to hear that the above groups of words are not complete sentences. However, you may have noticed that they would be complete sentences if you eliminated the underlined introductory words. Word groups such as the above are called *clauses.*

Clauses like these have a subject and a verb but depend on a complete sentence to finish the thought and cannot stand alone. Therefore, they are called *dependent clauses* or *subordinate clauses.* (Clauses that *can* stand alone as sentences are called *independent* clauses.)

Here is a partial list of introductory words that commonly begin subordinate clauses. They are, appropriately enough, called subordinating conjunctions:

after	as though	so (meaning *so that*)	until
although	because	so that	when
as	before	than	whenever
as if	even if	that	where
as long as	if	though	wherever
as soon as	since	unless	while

In the following sentences, the dependent clauses have been correctly attached to a complete sentence. Read the sentences aloud.

1. *Because college students deserve help with their writing, the university provides free tutoring in the Writing Lab.*
2. *Whenever you have writer's block, try making yourself freewrite for ten minutes.*
3. *You may find yourself actually enjoying writing if you consult with a tutor regularly.*

Notice:

*   When the dependent clause appears at the *beginning* of a sentence, a comma separates the dependent clause from the rest of the sentence.

- When the dependent clause comes at the *end* of the whole sentence, a comma is *not* used to separate it from the rest of the sentence.

Punctuating: Underline the dependent clauses in the following student-written sentences. Insert commas as needed.

Examples:

Whenever I eat pizza, I feel content.

I feel content whenever I eat pizza.

1. When I was a sophomore at Barberton High School I made the varsity basketball team.
2. I met my best friend when I was working at Johnson's Grocery Store.
3. Last night I felt as if I were in the middle of a gang war.
4. I hate to drive when it snows.
5. As long as the dog is a puppy he must be watched.
6. When it happens you'll know.
7. Unless he comes soon I will leave without him.
8. Li went to sleep before anyone else became even a little drowsy.
9. The store manager will not hire you unless you are really interested.
10. Although the movie was short it was very interesting.

Practice: The following sentences can be connected in a number of ways. See how many ways you can use a *subordinating conjunction* to connect them logically.

Here is a list of subordinating conjunctions:

after	as though	so (meaning *so that*)	until
although	because	so that	when
as	before	than	whenever
as if	even if	that	where
as long as	if	though	wherever
as soon as	since	unless	while

1. Alicia hurried to the drug store for a prescription.
   Her mother was sick.

   _____

   _____

2. I study and attend class regularly.
   I will probably get good grades this semester.

   _____

   _____

3. The movie was short.
   It was interesting.

   _____

   _____

4. My kids arrive home.
   They are ready for a snack.

   _____

   _____

5. My best friend was angry with me.
   I refused to go shopping with her.

   _____

   _____

6. We will study for the quiz together.
   We are sure to pass with flying colors.

   _____

   _____

7. My friend watched my books.

I went to the rest room.

_____

_____

8. I will meet you later.
   You have many things to do now.

_____

_____

9. You help Bob with his report.
   I will help Meko with her math.

_____

_____

10. I approached her room
    I didn't hear any music.

_____

_____

11. I waited for his phone call.
    We could discuss our homework.

_____

_____

12. I came back to school.
    I am tired of my dead-end job.

_____

_____

13. The tree fell onto his house.
    He had to buy a chainsaw.

_____

_____

14. People were looking at me.
    I was crazy.

_____

_____

15. The weekend comes.
    There isn't anything to do.

_____

_____

16. I apologized.
    I knew it didn't make up for everything.

_____

_____

17. The babysitter stayed overnight.
    We were not returning until the next day.

_____

_____

18. I never lock myself out of the house.
    I keep a spare key under the door mat.

_____

_____

19. I left for school.
    I realized that it was only Sunday.

_____

_____

20. We had been friends for a while.
    I noticed that he changed quite a bit.

_____

_____

Composing: Alone, with a partner, or in a group, brainstorm a list of personal accomplishments and disappointments that occurred during your first few weeks of college. Then construct ten sentences of your own, using a dependent clause and a main clause to show the relationship between your ideas.

Remember:

- Use a comma after a dependent clause that begins a sentence.
- Do not use a comma with a dependent clause that appears at the end of a sentence.

Possible exploration: Choose one or more of your composing sentences to inspire you as you freely write about a recent event in your life.

USING COORDINATION AND SUBORDINATION WITHIN A PARAGRAPH

You have practiced joining complete sentences and parts of sentences with coordinating conjunctions and with semicolons with and without transitional words. You have also practiced joining clauses to complete sentences with subordinating conjunctions. The punctuation of both the coordinating conjunctions and subordinating conjunctions depends on how or where the conjunctions are used.

Practice recognizing how coordination and subordination are used: Read aloud the following student draft. Now read it again and mark examples of coordinating conjunctions and subordinating conjunctions. Then discuss with your group why you think the student chose to use the conjunctions that appear. Notice the punctuation, too.

You may also wish to discuss other ways that the student might have combined sentences or might have otherwise improved this draft.

> *Jenny is my best friend. As I look at her picture, there are many words that come to mind. The one word that is repeated the most is* <u>*perfection*</u>*. She is 5'6" (the perfect height) and has long curly brown hair that is always perfect, and her face never has any blemishes.*
>
> *As I look farther down, I notice that familiar sparkling gold necklace with a tiny cross attached to it. If I had to think of a symbol to describe Jenny, it would be that necklace. Gold is one of the softest metals in the world, yet it is very precious. Jenny is not very strong physically, but mentally she is very strong. She always pushes herself to the farthest limits. She puts herself in situations where many of us would quit or give up; nevertheless, she puts up with it somehow and gets the job done.*
>
> *Like gold, Jenny is also very precious—not only to me but to everyone. I have never been as close to anyone as I am to her. She has given me a smile as bright as the sun and a shoulder to wipe my tears on. Even to a guy who doesn't express his feelings all that often, knowing that someone is there for you is something that is irreplaceable. She has given me more than I can ever repay. I'm not talking about money; I'm talking about the love that she has given to me.*

Composing: Use a draft of your own to practice using coordination and subordination.

1. Read through the draft and mark the coordinating conjunctions, the semicolons, and the subordinating conjunctions that you find

in it. Next, read aloud each sentence containing a conjunction or semicolon. Carefully correct any punctuation errors you find.

- Use commas before coordinating conjunctions that join complete sentences.

  Use commas at the end of subordinate clauses that *begin* sentences.

- Use a semicolon before and a comma after a transitional word that joins two complete sentences.

- Coordinating conjunctions that do not separate complete sentences *do not* require commas.

- *Do not* use commas before subordinate clauses that *end* sentences.

2. Reread your draft aloud and mark those sentences that might sound more effective if they were combined with coordinating conjunctions, with semicolons alone, with semicolons and transitional words, or with subordinating conjunctions.

   - Rewrite the sentences you chose, and then read your revised version of your draft aloud.

   - Notice how the revised sentences change the sound of your draft.

Possible exploration: "Cut a slice" out of the draft you used for the composing exercise and freely write in detail about the small section that you chose. Discuss the effectiveness of your "slice" with a partner or a group.

Alternate exploration: Perhaps you now see things differently than when you first wrote the draft you used for this exercise. If so, freely write about how you now feel. Include *why* you changed your mind.

USING RELATIVE CLAUSES TO ADD DETAILS

You may remember from the section on subordination that although a dependent clause has a subject and a verb, it cannot stand alone as a sentence. A relative clause is a special kind of dependent clause.

A relative clause is used as an adjective and normally follows the noun that it modifies. Relative clauses usually begin with a relative pronoun.

Here are some common relative pronouns:

that   which   who   whose   whom

Some of the following relative clauses might sound all right if they were questions or if they were answers to questions. Read them aloud as simple declarative sentences and notice that they do not make sense when read alone. They are properly used immediately after the nouns or pronouns they describe.

1. *that I am going to buy when I get paid*
2. *who warned me about the detour*
3. *whose style I admire*
4. *which I have watched ever since I was a child*

When you speak, you probably have little trouble with relative clauses; but when you are writing, you want to be as clear as possible for your readers.

Here are some possible ways to use the above relative clauses. Notice that some of the underlined clauses may be punctuated more than one way. *Punctuation is to help the reader;* therefore, the *writer* decides what the sentence means and then punctuates it to help the reader understand.

1. I just found the stereo amplifier <u>that I am going to buy when I get paid.</u>
2a. The police officer <u>who warned me about the detour</u> received an award for public service.
2b. Officer Washington, <u>who warned me about the detour,</u> received an award for public service.
3a. The professor <u>whose style I admire</u> just received a promotion.
3b. Dr. Redmond, <u>whose style I admire,</u> just received a promotion.
4. The Star Trek movies and television series, <u>which I have watched ever since I was a child,</u> have more followers than ever.

The purpose of the following lessons is to help you make well-informed choices about your writing.

USING RELATIVE CLAUSES BEGINNING WITH *THAT* THAT <u>DO NOT</u> REQUIRE COMMAS

In everyday speech and writing we use clauses beginning with *that* to describe things or people. For example:

1a. The radio was very expensive.

The radio played the loud music.

These sentences can be combined to read:

1b. The radio <u>that played the loud music</u> was very expensive. OR

The radio <u>that was very expensive</u> played loud music.

2a. I will marry a person.

The person will be compassionate.

These sentences can be combined to read:

2b. The person <u>that I marry</u> will be compassionate. OR

I will marry a person <u>that is compassionate.</u>

Notice:

- Relative clauses come immediately after the noun or pronoun that they describe.
- Relative clauses that begin with the word *that* are *not* separated from the rest of the sentence by commas because they contain *information that is needed to identify the words they describe.*

Read the following sentences aloud and notice how the relative clauses are needed to identify the words they describe. Discuss how the meaning of the words *room, book,* and *accident* would change if the information in the relative clause were different.

1. *The room <u>that is reserved for smokers</u> is around the corner.*
2. *The book <u>that the teacher assigned</u> is quite lengthy.*
3. *The car accident <u>that injured my friend</u> was caused by slick roads.*

Hint: *Do not* use a comma before the word *that!*

Practice: Work with a partner to combine the following pairs of sentences by turning one into a relative clause beginning with *that*. Notice that most of these sentences can be combined at least two effective ways, depending on what the writer wants to emphasize.

1. The car was driven by a drunk driver.
   The car hit the little girl.

   _____

   _____

2. The folder contained important papers.
   The folder was missing.

   _____

   _____

3. The electric guitar had a great sound.
   I bought the guitar at a pawn shop.

   _____

   _____

4. I attempted to avoid the potholes.
   The potholes were in the middle of the
   street.

   _____

   _____

5. The team filed a protest with the
   commissioner.
   The team lost the game.

   _____

   _____

6. The house belonged to my best friend.
   The house caught on fire.

   _____

   _____

7. The car is shiny red.
   My mother bought the car.

   _____

   _____

8. The device is broken.
   The device controls my computer's disk drive.

   _____

   _____

9. The time will benefit others.
   We spend the time on charitable activities.

   _____

   _____

10. Alice Walker wrote the book.
    The book is a good one to read.

    _____

    _____

11. Toni Morrison is a Nobel Prize winner.
    The winner grew up in Ohio.

    _____

    _____

12. The first time I drank was a terrible experience.
    I will never forget the experience.

    _____

    _____

13. Part of the house will take a year to rebuild.

That part was struck by lightning.

_____

_____

14. The tall, athletic-looking man turned out to be Michael Jordan.
    The man appeared in expensive clothing.

    _____

    _____

15. The football team won the game.
    The team was expected to lose the game.

    _____

    _____

16. The professional athlete does outstanding work during the game.
    The athlete trains every day.

    _____

    _____

17. The necklace hangs down his neck.
    The necklace has a large letter J on it.

    _____

    _____

18. Those clouds might bring us some rain.
    Those clouds are black.

    _____

    _____

19. The expensive shoes went on sale two days later.

Everyone wanted the shoes.

_____

_____

20. The new computer is faster than mine.
    My nephew bought the computer.

_____

_____

Composing: Work with a partner or in a group. Look around your classroom as you brainstorm a list of things you might describe. Use your list as you write ten sentences vividly describing things around you. Include relative clauses beginning with _that_ in each sentence.

Possible exploration: Choose one or two things from your list of classroom objects to freewrite about in detail. Use your imagination. Perhaps create a fantasy. Perhaps be more serious and analyze just _why_ classrooms are arranged as they are. In either case, allow your mind to roam free. You do not have to come to any conclusions. Just explore.

USING RELATIVE CLAUSES BEGINNING WITH *WHO* THAT <u>DO NOT</u> REQUIRE COMMAS

You are probably familiar with clauses that begin with the word *who*. All relative clauses beginning with *who*, like some relative clauses beginning with *that*, are used to describe people. The relative clauses appear immediately after the word that they describe. For example:

1a. He was the man.

   The man helped me fix my tire.

These sentences can be combined to read:

1b. He was the man *that helped me fix my tire.* OR

   He was the man *who helped me fix my tire.*

2a. There is the mail carrier.

   The mail carrier gave my dog a treat.

These sentences can be combined to read:

2b. There is the mail carrier *that gave my dog a treat.* OR

   There is the mail carrier *who gave my dog a treat.*

Punctuation: Like relative clauses beginning with *that*, this type of descriptive clause is *not* separated from the rest of the sentence by commas because it contains information that is needed to identify the person it describes.

Read the following sentences aloud and notice how the relative clauses are needed to identify the words they describe. Discuss how the meaning of the words *person, anyone,* and *student* would change if the information in the relative clause were different.

1.   *The person <u>who taught Kevin how to use a computer</u> is now a millionaire.*
2.   *I will always be grateful to anyone <u>who helps me learn a new skill.</u>*
3.   *Antiwan is the type of student <u>who is never afraid to ask a question.</u>*

Practice: Combine the following pairs of sentences by turning one into a relative clause beginning with *who*. You decide which sentence becomes the relative clause, depending on what you want to emphasize.

```
1. The woman pushed her way onto the bus again
   today.
   She was rude to me yesterday.
```

_____

_____

2. People are really gross.
   People throw their cigarette butts on the
   ground.

   _____

   _____

3. Some women are as strong as men.
   Some women play football.

   _____

   _____

4. The guest stole our silverware.
   The guest came to dinner last Saturday.

   _____

   _____

5. Students will not succeed in college.
   Students play cards in the lounge all day.

   _____

   _____

6. Andre was the only friend.
   The friend really cared about me when my
   parents divorced.

   _____

   _____

7. Tamara is a remarkable woman.
   The woman meets with a self-help group
   weekly.

_____

_____

8. There I was, searching for love, affection, and support from a woman.
   The woman never knew how to love herself.

_____

_____

9. The woman hit a rabbit that was crossing the road.
   The woman was driving a pick-up truck.

_____

_____

10. My friend stayed the weekend with me.
    My friend helped me move into my new apartment.

_____

_____

11. Jenny is one person in my past.
    The person in my past influenced me to see the good in people.

_____

_____

12. Students will be in good shape.
    The students jog two miles every day.

_____

_____

13. I do not like to go out with people.

The people act immaturely.

_____

_____

14. The good-looking teenager smiled at the girl
    across the room.
    The teenager was standing by the punch bowl.

_____

_____

15. I liked the song even though I didn't know
    the musician.
    The musician sang it.

_____

_____

16. The man smelled like my favorite cologne.
    The man sat behind me in writing class.

_____

_____

17. Irresponsible drivers should have to serve
    time in jail.
    Irresponsible drivers drive drunk.

_____

_____

18. The car belonged to a citizen.
    The citizen left it sitting on the side of
    the road for a week.

_____

_____

19. The runner went to the hospital for
    treatment.
    The runner was injured during practice.

    _____

    _____

20. The athlete wants to defend his title this
    year.
    The athlete is the 200 meter state champion.

    _____

    _____

Composing: Brainstorm a list of the *kinds* of people that you meet
every day. Use your list to help you write ten sentences using relative
clauses beginning with *who* that are needed to identify a person.

For this exercise:

* Place the relative clause immediately after the word that it
  describes.
* Do not *name* a person in these sentences.
* Do not use commas to separate the relative clause from the rest of
  the sentence.

Possible exploration: Use one or more of your composing sentences to
explore your thoughts as you freewrite about one or more types of
people. Then discuss your freewriting with a partner or group, pay-
ing special attention to how much of your freewriting is based on pre-
conceptions or stereotypes and how much is based on your personal
experience with individuals.

USING RELATIVE CLAUSES BEGINNING WITH *WHO* THAT REQUIRE COMMAS

When you use a relative clause beginning with *who* to add information about a person, you may find that, although the clause adds interesting information, it is not really needed to *identify* the person it describes. For example:

1a. Erika Jones is now the branch manager.
    She started in the mail room.

These sentences can be combined to read:

1b. Erika Jones, <u>who started in the mail room,</u> is now the branch manager. OR
    Erika Jones, <u>who is now the branch manager,</u> started in the mail room.
2a. My mother is attending college.
    My mother wants to become a lawyer.

These sentences can be combined to read:

2b. My mother, <u>who is attending college,</u> wants to become a lawyer. OR
    My mother, <u>who wants to become a lawyer,</u> is attending college.

In the above examples we do not need the relative clause to *identify* Erika or my mother because the person's name (*Erika*) or other positive identification (*my mother*) are in the main clause. In cases like this, the relative clause should be set off from the rest of the sentence by a comma or by a set of commas.

Punctuation: Read each of the following student-written sentences aloud to help you hear the pattern of this kind of relative clause. Insert commas to separate the relative clause from the rest of the sentence.

```
1. Reggie White who plays defensive line for the
   Green Bay Packers signed a multimillion
   dollar contract for five years.
2. My favorite teacher who lectures every day
   taught us about oxidation reduction.
3. Dawn and Kristy who go to Kent State will
   soon transfer to our university.
4. The Bears who are 5 and 6 are not going to
   the Super Bowl.
```

5. My oldest brother whom I like a lot is always there when I need someone to talk to.
6. Jason who has a drinking problem started attending AA meetings.
7. My father who is a large man loves to eat.
8. My mother's only brother who works in the steel mill is a great mechanic.
9. Lori who is in my Basic Writing class will be in my First Aid class next semester.
10. Michelle who is my sister is a model for *Vogue* magazine.

Practice: Combine the following sentences by turning one into a relative clause beginning with *who* and separating it from the rest of the sentence with commas. Remember to place the relative clause immediately after the word that it describes.

1. I told my mom about my hangover.
   My mom was not very sympathetic.

   _____

   _____

2. My father was disappointed when I dropped out of school.
   My father always wanted to be an engineer.

   _____

   _____

3. Valerie will probably not make the cheerleading squad.
   Valerie has two left feet.

   _____

   _____

4. Kurt is not welcome in our home.
   Kurt smokes marijuana all the time.

_____

_____

5. My roommate had the nerve to ask me to clean
   up my area.
   He always throws his dirty socks in the
   closet.

   _____

   _____

6. B Dog was arrested for carrying a gun without
   a license.
   B Dog is the neighborhood drug dealer.

   _____

   _____

7. My mother cooked steak last night.
   My mother is usually concerned about our
   health.

   _____

   _____

8. My best fried got the highest grade in the
   class.
   She studied for weeks for the final exam.

   _____

   _____

9. I am excited because my big brother will be
   coming home in June.
   My brother is in the Navy.

   _____

   _____

10. Sam threw oranges at stop signs until he was issued a $50 fine.
    Sam is my best friend.

    _____

    _____

11. Nicole is exciting to go out with.
    Nicole is studying marine biology.

    _____

    _____

12. Mr. Walker works in the Math Lab.
    Mr. Walker also teaches several Basic Math classes.

    _____

    _____

13. My brother does not care about anyone but himself.
    My brother is a real jerk.

    _____

    _____

14. Julie spends a lot of time with her boyfriend.
    Julie is one of my closest friends.

    _____

    _____

15. Frank never wants to go out to look for a job.
    Frank is inexplicably lazy.

    _____

    _____

Composing: As a class or with a partner or a group, brainstorm a list of specific people; include friends, family members, public figures, or others. Use your list to help you write ten sentences, each containing a relative clause beginning with *who* that requires commas. Remember to place the relative clause immediately after the specific person that it describes.

Possible exploration: Choose one or two people from the sentences you wrote. Brainstorm a detailed list of characteristics that you may attribute to the person(s). Share your list with a partner or group. Help each other add details to your lists as you discuss the complexity of individual personalities.

USING RELATIVE CLAUSES BEGINNING WITH *WHICH* THAT REQUIRE COMMAS

In your speaking and writing you may also be familiar with clauses that begin with the word *which*. Notice how the following sentences can be combined.

1a. The library's computer lab is available to all university students.
     The library's computer lab is on the third floor.

These sentences can be combined to read:

1b. The library's computer lab, <u>which is on the third floor,</u> is available to all university students.
2a. I am going to rent *Casablanca*.
     Casablanca is my favorite movie.

These sentences can be combined to read:

2b. I am going to rent *Casablanca*, <u>which is my favorite movie.</u>

Notice:

- As with all relative clauses, this kind of clause appears immediately after the word that it describes.
- A relative clause beginning with *which* can be set off from the rest of the sentence by a comma or by a set of commas. The commas are used when the clause is not necessary to identify the word it describes.

The following student-written sentences are correct, except that the punctuation has been omitted. Read each sentence aloud to help you hear the pattern of these clauses. Then insert a comma or commas to separate the relative clause from the rest of the sentence.

1. My house which was the oldest on the street recently burned down.
2. Diving which is a very difficult sport takes hours of practice.
3. Beer drinking which is a popular college habit is not good for your health.
4. My dad works for General Motors which employs many workers.

5. Howard University which my sister attends is a fine school.

6. My sociology term paper which was very important to me was stolen yesterday.

7. I have a Geo Tracker which is a mini-jeep.

8. Bill Walsh Football which is a Sega Genesis game is very exciting to play.

9. We were playing soccer in the snow which added to the numbness of my body.

10. Michigan State soccer team which won its league title did not qualify for the NCAA Tournament.

Practice: Combine the following sentences by turning one into a relative clause beginning with *which* and separating it from the rest of the sentence with a comma or a set of commas. You will notice that a number of sentences can be combined in different ways, depending on what you wish to emphasize.

1. My '78 Mustang is an awesome machine.
   My '78 Mustang is my pride and joy.

   _____

   _____

2. I got in trouble for nodding off in class.
   It is something I hardly ever do.

   _____

   _____

3. Coffee puts me to sleep.
   Coffee can usually keep you awake all night.

   _____

   _____

4. Joseph is my middle name.
   Joseph is also my father's name.

   _____

   _____

5. His strong upper body is due to the work he does at the factory.
   His upper body makes him look like a body builder.

   _____

   _____

6. Memorial Hall is considered to be the center of the campus.
   Memorial Hall has white pillars.

   _____

   _____

7. The bulldog was picked up by the dog pound because it didn't have a license.
   The bulldog belonged to Henry.

   _____

   _____

8. Tomatoes make me sick.
   Tomatoes were on my hamburger.

   _____

   _____

9. My favorite chair looks old and dirty.
   My favorite chair is very comfortable.

   _____

   _____

10. I was angry when my new textbook fell into the mud puddle.
    My textbook cost forty-five dollars.

    _____

    _____

11. Our small jet experienced a bumpy landing.
    The landing made me hit my head on the ceiling.

    _____

    _____

12. The corner gas station will have to undergo many repairs.
    The gas station will be closed during December.

    _____

    _____

13. The circus will be the main attraction in our town this week.
    The circus comes only once a year.

    _____

    _____

14. State's football team is not going to make it this year.
    State's football team had a chance for the Las Vegas Bowl last year.

    _____

    _____

15. Crack causes people to die quickly.
    Crack is an illegal drug.

    _____

    _____

Composing: With a partner or in a group, brainstorm a list of ten *things* or *activities* that are of interest to you. Write a sentence about each item. Include a properly punctuated relative clause beginning with *which* in each sentence.

Possible exploration: Choose one of your favorite possessions or favorite pastimes to freewrite about in detail. Describe the possession or the pastime, but be sure to include how it makes you feel and *why* it makes you feel that way.

USING OTHER DESCRIPTIVE ELEMENTS

USING APPOSITIVES IN WRITING

You have been practicing punctuating relative clauses, which you regularly use in both speaking and writing. By now, sentences such as the following (with relative clauses underlined) should look fairly familiar to you:

1. Luis, <u>who was the mystery pizza-lover,</u> ate my pizza.
2. Chicken, <u>which is my favorite food,</u> is good for me.
3. Many people also love Joe's favorite food, <u>which is tacos.</u>

Sometimes writers want to compress relative clauses into a written form that we often see in print but rarely use in everyday conversation. This form is called an appositive. Like a relative clause, it renames the noun immediately before it, and it is often set off from the rest of the sentence by a comma or commas.

Here are the example sentences rewritten to contain appositives. The appositives have been underlined and an arrow has been drawn to the word that they rename.

1. Luis, <u>the mystery pizza-lover</u>, ate my pizza.

2. Chicken, <u>my favorite food,</u> is good for me.

3. Many people also love Joe's favorite food, <u>tacos.</u>

Notice:

- The appositive comes immediately after the word that it renames.
- The appositive is set off from the rest of the sentence by one or more commas.
- The appositive *does not contain a verb.* It is a noun phrase.

Punctuating: The following student-written sentences contain appositives. Underline the appositive and insert commas to set off the appositive from the rest of the sentence.

1. Rodney my brother was in the army and was stationed in Frankfurt.
2. Jeff my friend could always be recognized by his blue jeans and preppy sweaters.

3. It hit me that I was in the red-light district the worst place in the city.

4. The day was December 21, 1991 the last day before Christmas vacation.

5. He introduced me to Sergeant Wicker the fist woman Marine I met.

6. I picked Maroud Jackson a friend from high school.

7. Everyone stood in line to use the same restroom a regular stall.

8. This was my dream my goal!

9. I will always remember my father the little short man with the belly like St. Nick as the thin young man he once was.

10. My favorite food lobster is very expensive.

Practice: Combine each group of the following student-written sentences to form one sentence that contains an appositive. These sentences may be combined in more than one way. Use your discretion as to which sentence becomes the appositive and which one stays a complete sentence.

1. Jerry is my best friend.
   Jerry is one of the craziest people I know.

   _____

   _____

2. My neighbors allow me to use their phone.
   My neighbors are Ivan, Jamal, and Shock.

   _____

   _____

3. I will be 22 years old on my next birthday.
   My birthday is July 22.

   _____

   _____

4. She introduced me to her mother.

Her mother is Jessie.
Jessie is the lady that raised her.

_____

_____

5. Anthony ordered the dishwashers to clean the ovens.
   Anthony is the head chef.

_____

_____

6. Nancy cried when she didn't get her way.
   Nancy is a spoiled child.

_____

_____

7. Yumeko rushed to the door to keep the robbers out.
   Yumeko is the security officer.

_____

_____

8. Ramone now lives at my house.
   Ramone is Jessica's boyfriend.

_____

_____

9. I went on my favorite ride ten times.
   My favorite ride is the roller coaster.

_____

_____

10. Gerry often visits "study table" to make sure
    that the athletes are doing their homework.
    Gerry is the head coach.

    _____

    _____

11. Kelly decided we would meet at the barn at
    noon.
    Kelly is my good friend and hunting partner.

    _____

    _____

12. My Writing Lab tutor has a good personality.
    Steve is my Writing Lab tutor.

    _____

    _____

13. My brother's wife is going to have a baby.
    My brother's wife's name is Heidi.

    _____

    _____

14. My sweet stereo can loudly thump my bass
    speakers.
    My stereo is a Pioneer 7460 tuner.

    _____

    _____

15. Brandon smoothly tossed me a piece of gum.
    Brandon was the cool guy in the class.

    _____

    _____

16. R & B Soul is an essential part of my everyday life.

    R & B Soul is a relaxing, joyous form of music.

    _____

    _____

17. My pet frog escaped from his tank.

    My pet frog is named Willy.

    _____

    _____

18. My sister's little black book had some juicy stories.

    My sister's little black book was her diary.

    _____

    _____

19. Taz is my Siamese kitten.

    Taz is very rambunctious.

    _____

    _____

20. I made it through "Hell Week."

    "Hell Week" is the first week of Navy Seal training.

    _____

    _____

Composing exercise #1:   Look back at the "Composing" sentences you wrote for the lessons about relative clauses that *required commas.* Choose ten of these sentences that would be appropriate to rewrite with appositives. Rewrite them and then read them aloud; notice how using appositives affects their sound.

Composing exercise #2: Choose a freewriting or a draft that you have written. Read through it twice before deciding whether there might be appropriate places to add appositives. Rewrite the sentences that seem suitable for appositives. Discuss how adding appositives affects the draft.

USING PARTICIPLES AS SINGLE-WORD MODIFIERS

In speaking, and more often in writing, we sometimes use especially colorful descriptive words called *participles.* The underlined participles in the following sentences are used as adjectives to describe nouns. Read the sentences aloud.

1. *In the middle of my hike in the canyon, I was nearly hit by a <u>falling</u> rock.*
2. *The <u>singing</u> bird woke me up even before sunrise.*
3. *The <u>frightened puppy</u> ran away.*
4. *I had a difficult time calming down the <u>frustrated</u> customer.*

In sentences 1 and 2 above, *falling* describes *rock* and *singing* describes *bird.* In sentences 3 and 4, *frightened* describes *puppy* and *frustrated* describes *customer.*

PRESENT PARTICIPLES, such as *falling* and *singing,* are the base form of a verb with an -*ing* ending added.

PAST PARTICIPLES such as *frightened* and *frustrated,* are the base form of a verb with a past tense ending added.

Using *Present* Participles as Single-Word Modifiers

Establishing the pattern: To help you get the "sound" of the pattern of a participle used as a single-word modifier, work with a partner to make a long list of present participles paired with nouns. You will use this list later. To help you maintain the pattern, use the word *the* or the word *a* before the participle.

Here are some student examples to get you started. See how long you can make your own list of noun phrases as you brainstorm with your partner for five minutes.

the falling rock	the burning candle	a leaping lizard
the crying baby	a roaring sound	the running engine
_____	_____	_____
_____	_____	_____
_____	_____	_____
_____	_____	_____
_____	_____	_____

Practice: Combine the following sentences. Your completed sentence should have at least one present participle used as a modifier.

1. The dog frightened off the burglar.
   The dog was barking.

   _____

   _____

2. The hiker was killed by a rock.
   The rock was falling.

   _____

   _____

3. Max Headroom was only a head.
   The head is talking.

   _____

   _____

4. I love all the birds that surround my house
   in the spring.
   The birds are singing.

   _____

   _____

5. Tamara wished on a star and became a
   famous poet.
   The star was shining.

   _____

   _____

6. The patient needed much attention.
   The patient was gasping.

   _____

   _____

7. The rain ruined my whole day.
   The rain was pouring down.

   _____

   _____

8. Buzzards waited patiently to spot the remains
   of another animal's kill.
   The buzzards were circling.
   The remains were decaying.

   _____

   _____

9. A girl slammed the door after her boyfriend
   dumped her.
   The girl was raging.

   _____

   _____

10. The fire fighter emerged from the house.
    The house was flaming.

    _____

    _____

11. The dog was just a figment of his
    imagination.
    The dog could talk.

    _____

    _____

12. The patient was so sick that he could barely
    eat his food.
    The patient had a cough.

    _____

    _____

13. The sun cheered us all up.
    The sun was shining brightly.

    _____

    _____

14. The dog was tired from chasing the ball.
    The dog was panting.

    _____

    _____

15. The sound of the tornado made us all panic.
    The sound roared.

    _____

    _____

Composing: Use your list of noun phrases to help you create ten sentences using present participles as modifiers right before nouns.

Remember:

- Use your noun phrases just as they are. Don't move the participle to another place in your sentence.
- Your sentence will have a verb *in addition to* the participle that appears right before the noun.

USING *PAST* PARTICIPLES AS SINGLE-WORD MODIFIERS

The past participles in the following sentences are underlined. Read the sentences aloud.

1. *The <u>frightened</u> puppy ran away.*
2. *I had a difficult time calming down the <u>frustrated</u> customer.*
3. *The <u>frozen</u> fish thawed out when our freezer became unplugged.*
4. *All that was left of my collection were a few <u>broken</u> records.*

PAST PARTICIPLES, such as the words *frightened* and *frustrated,* are the base form of a verb with a past tense ending added. The usual past tense ending, of course, is *-ed.* However, some irregular verbs such as *frozen* and *broken* form their past participles with an *-en* ending. These words may also be used as single-word modifiers before a noun.

Establishing the pattern: As with present participles, it is good to get used to the "sound pattern" of past participles used as single-word modifiers. Here are some student examples of phrases that begin with the words *the* or *a,* use a past participle as a modifier, and end with a noun.

Work with a partner to make your own list of noun phrases as you brainstorm for five minutes.

the educated student   the burnt toast
the fallen rock   the well-lighted room
the collapsed house   the roasted meat

_____   _____

_____   _____

_____   _____

_____   _____

_____   _____

_____   _____

_____   _____

_____   _____

Practice: Combine the following sentences so that your completed sentences each have at least one past participle used as a modifier.

1. Mary's job at the store is to stack the vegetables on the shelf.
   The vegetables are canned.

   _____

   _____

2. The money could not be spent.
   The money was marked.

   _____

   _____

3. After waiting all afternoon, my friends and I enjoyed eating the pig.
   The pig was roasted.

   _____

   _____

4. I cried as my truck was towed away.
   My truck was smashed.

   _____

   _____

5. We were all a little nervous as we watched the sky.
   The sky was darkly clouded.

   _____

   _____

6. I was not able to get the mustard out of my jeans.
   The mustard was dried.
   My jeans were stained.

   _____

   _____

7. Loretta smiled nervously as she entered the room.
   The room was brightly lighted.

   _____

   _____

8. Tony helped himself to Shannon's salad.
   The salad was tossed.

   _____

   _____

9. We watched the veterinarian fix the tiger's tooth.
   The veterinarian was well-respected.
   The tiger was drugged.

   _____

   _____

10. The convict broke into the store in search of the safe.
    The convict had escaped.
    The store was unguarded.
    The safe was hidden.

    _____

    _____

Composing: Use your list of noun phrases to help you create ten sentences using past participles as modifiers right before nouns.

Remember:

- Use your noun phrases just as they are. Don't move the participle to another place in your sentence.
- Your sentence will have a verb _in addition to_ the participle that appears right before the noun.

USING PARTICIPIAL *PHRASES* AS MODIFIERS

You have probably noticed that participles used as single-word modifiers are a lot like adjectives, only they describe *and* show action at the same time. Participles are very versatile, and we will now add another way for you to use them as modifiers.

You can use participial PHRASES as modifiers to show even more action! As before, we will work with descriptive participial phrases in two tenses: (1) present participial phrases and (2) past participial phrases.

Using *Present* Participial Phrases as Modifiers

The present participial phrases in the following sentences have been underlined. Read the sentences aloud.

1. *Dripping with bubbling cheese, the pizza was so hot that it burned my tongue.*
2. *The waiter, leaving the customers to enjoy an evening of feasting, walked quietly away.*
3. *Yvette, always thinking quickly, didn't even lose her place in the book.*
4. *Calming his nerves by breathing slowly, Morris walked into the classroom to give a speech.*

Notice:

- The participial phrase begins with a participle or with an adverb that modifies the participle, as in sentence 3 above.
- The participial phrase is placed *next to* the word that it describes.
- The phrase is often separated from the rest of the sentence by a comma or a set of commas.

Punctuating: With a partner or in a group, read each of the following student-written sentences aloud. Then underline the present participial phrases and insert commas as needed.

1. I opened the flap to the tent and left by myself leaving the others behind as they were getting ready.
2. Becoming disgusted after stopping twice for directions I parked my car and hailed a cab.
3. I silently followed her anxiously waiting to see what would happen next.

4. I was quite bored with looking at the mountains knowing I had many more miles to go.

5. Depending on the terrain features we could see thirty miles in any given direction.

6. The audience responded with a sea of fire holding lighters in the air.

7. Mike not thinking right left the scene of the accident.

8. Running and dodging players the forward went straight for the goal.

9. Hoping it wouldn't rain I left my umbrella in my hall closet.

10. The marathon runner crying from the pain continued to run the last mile.

Practice: Combine the following sentences, turning at least one of them into a present participial phrase. You decide which of the sentences should become the participial phrase. Many of them can be written more than one way.

Remember:

* Begin the phrase with a participle or an adverb that modifies the participle.
* Place the phrase *next to* the word that it describes.
* Use a comma or commas to separate the participial phrase from the rest of the sentence.

1. Autumn finished the haircut quickly.
   Autumn continued to smile at the rude woman.

   _____

   _____

2. The teacher bored the class.
   The teacher lectured endlessly.

   _____

   _____

3. Dan tackled a player.
   Dan broke his leg.

_____

_____

4. The wind storm blew in from the north.
   The wind storm caused the boat to tip on
   its side.

_____

_____

5. The split end ran for a touchdown.
   The split end received the ball.

_____

_____

6. I was zigging and zagging.
   I chased sea gulls all over the beach.

_____

_____

7. George moved quickly.
   George pushed me out of the way.

_____

_____

8. The baseball player darted toward second base.
   The baseball player focused on the pitcher.

_____

_____

9. The kids couldn't get any sleep.
   The kids were thinking about the concert.

_____

_____

```
10. The cheerleaders jumped up and down.
    The cheerleaders charmed the fans.
```

_____

_____

Composing: Think of an interesting event that you have witnessed or in which you have participated, such as lunch hour in the student union, a party, a wedding, or a holiday event. First brainstorm a list of the *actions* that occurred during the event. Then write five to ten sentences about the event, including at least one present participial phrase in each sentence. Do not worry about writing an organized paragraph.

Possible exploration: "Cut a slice" from the event you wrote about for the Composing exercise. Include physical details and personal reactions related to the one limited moment you choose to write about.

USING *PAST* PARTICIPIAL PHRASES AS MODIFIERS

A phrase that begins with a *past* participle may also be used as a descriptive element in a sentence. The past participial phrases in the following sentences have been underlined. Read the sentences aloud.

1. *Disgusted after stopping twice for directions,* I parked my car and hailed a cab.
2. *Bored with looking at the mountains,* I started calculating how long the trip would take.
3. Aaron, *determined to pass his final,* studied all night.
4. The new college student, *encouraged by good grades,* decided to continue to study hard for tests.
5. The bottle, *frozen solid,* had been left in the deep freeze all night.

Notice:

- The participial phrase begins with a participle.
- The participial phrase is placed *next to* the word that it describes.
- The phrase is often separated from the rest of the sentence by a comma or a set of commas.

Punctuating: With a partner or in a group, read each of the following student-written sentences aloud. Then underline the participial phrases and insert commas as needed.

1. Flipped on its side the car started to burn.
2. The peanuts covered with ants were inedible.
3. Worried about school I went to get tutoring help.
4. Disgusted with girls he didn't go out on a date for a whole week.
5. Anthony excited about the grade he received on his speech told his friends that he was going out to celebrate.
6. Marie angered about her work schedule called in sick today.
7. Excited about Christmas I went shopping at Tower City.
8. The coach pleased with his team's performance congratulated his players in the locker room.
9. Excited about the party I was dressed hours ahead of time.

10. Awakened by the noise I jumped out of bed to see what it was.

Practice: Use any of the sentence-combining techniques that you know to combine the following sentences. Turn at least one of the sentences into a *past* participial phrase.

Remember:

- Begin the participial phrase with a participle or an adverb that modifies the participle.
- Place the phrase *next to* the word that it describes.
- Use a comma or commas to separate the participial phrase from the rest of the sentence.

1. The student was disgusted.
   The student was tired of homework.
   The student went to bed.

   _____

   _____

2. I was undecided where to go.
   I finally packed my bags.
   I headed for Florida for spring break.

   _____

   _____

3. The car door was frozen from the icy rain.
   The car door was hard to get open.

   _____

   _____

4. Bobby was stranded by the side of the road.
   Bobby fell asleep while waiting for help.

   _____

   _____

5. The child was frightened by the dog.
   The child screamed.
   The child cried for his mother.

   _____

   _____

6. The ground glistened under the bright full
   moon.
   The ground was covered with fresh white snow.

   _____

   _____

7. The car ended up stuck in the deep, muddy
   ditch.
   The car was driven by a twelve year old.

   _____

   _____

8. The writing teacher was pleased with the
   class' progress.
   The writing teacher gave them the rest of the
   day off with no homework.

   _____

   _____

9. Candi was not about to give up yet.
   Candi was thrown from the horse.

   _____

   _____

10. I was pleased with the hotel room.
    I gave the bellhop a big tip.

    _____

    _____

Composing: Work with a partner to create ten colorful sentences that use past participial phrases.

1. To help you get started, you may choose appropriate past participles from the following list, *Or* you may prefer to brainstorm a list of other past participles.
2. Remember to put the participle at the beginning of the descriptive phrase.
3. Place the phrase *next to* the noun or pronoun that it describes.
4. Use a comma or a set of commas to separate the participial phrase from the rest of the sentence.

Here are some past participles to get you started:

neglected	embarrassed	smashed	pleased
overlooked	annoyed	delighted	burnt
disgusted	crushed	satisfied	confused
frustrated	excited	irritated	decorated
rewarded	contented	trapped	
thrilled	frozen	misunderstood	
stained	criticized	puzzled	

Editing

*I*n the first two sections of this book we worked on fluency (discovering and focusing ideas) and sentence combining (gaining control in writing sentences). Now it is time to select some of your work for editing in order to prepare it for presentation.

SELECTING DRAFTS FOR YOUR PORTFOLIO

At this point you probably have a number of compositions that are coming together in some kind of focus, but some are not, and yet they may be interesting. First, try to arrange your work in the order that you wrote them, and then read everything through to get some idea of how far you have come as a writer. Don't throw anything away.

Feedback from other writers is important in helping you select your best work, so your instructor may want to put you in groups for reading and revision. Because other writers may not feel the same way you do about your favorite work, each writer should read several different pieces.

Openly discuss your reasons for selection, especially if you have different opinions. Remember, at this point you are writing for an audience.

Prioritizing

Identify each piece that you read to your group with a clear title. Each member of your group should then list on a piece of paper his or her order of preference and why. This is valuable feedback and will help you make your decisions.

Although a writer should always consider the audience, keep in mind that these lists are your classmates' subjective reactions. You are the final judge of which papers to revise.

Using a Descriptive Outline to Check for Focus

Choose a draft that you have written, and read it aloud to yourself. After you have read it, consider the main idea. Write the main idea on a separate piece of paper to use as a worksheet.

Now reread your paper and consider each block of information that seems to be about the same thing. Under the main idea on your worksheet, write what you did in the text. For example, "In the first two sentences I describe my father." Eventually you will have a list of descriptive phrases under the main idea. For example:

Main idea: My father was the most influential person in my life.

1. I introduce the topic

2. I describe my father

3. I tell the story of the first time driving the car.

4. I talk about my father's heart attack.

5. I sum up and restate the main idea that my father was a big influence.

Now ask yourself these questions about your descriptive phrases:

Why did I put this part here?
Would it be better somewhere else?
Does it even belong in this paper?

You may find yourself reacting as follows: *Wait a minute. The heart attack, although an interesting story, may not belong here. It might make another good paper. I think I'll edit it out of this one. In place of the material about the heart attack, maybe I should add another example of how my father influenced me.*

Before you continue on, try this procedure with a group. Read the following student-written draft aloud.

My Grandfather

I chose to describe my grandfather because he is a caring and giving man. My grandfather is a typical old man: he is about 5'6" tall and has a large stomach and wears his pants around his chest. He goes to bed early and gets up early. His appetite must be huge because he is always eating; his concerns lie on when the next meal is. He is a true old-timer. He believes that a man's hair shouldn't be worn long; this is evident in his own quarter-inch long, silver gray hair. He believes that to accomplish something you have to work hard at it or it really isn't worth having. Ever since I can remember, he has always had a dog and miscellaneous farm animals, such as chickens, ducks, rabbits, pigs, and even a skunk. My grandfather has many wrinkles in his face and hands and many worry lines across the forehead. If I had ten children, I think I would always look concerned, too. My grandfather has always been a hard worker. I can't remember ever seeing him without his work boots on and dirt under his fingernails. My grandfather is an old and beaten man with great amounts of pride. He holds his head high whenever he speaks of his family and their accomplishments.

Now practice writing a descriptive outline with your group.

1. Write the main idea at the top of a piece of paper.
2. Under the main idea, list in order the things that the writer *does* in the paper.
3. Discuss what parts you would move, change, or omit.
4. What other suggestions do you have for revision?

Compare your group's suggestions with other groups in the class.

Now try the procedure with your own paper. Work alone or with a partner. Then rewrite your draft, concentrating on making sure that all sentences contribute to the focus of your paper.

Responding to Your Text as a Reader

You can check your draft for integrity in many ways. Following is a checklist developed by an instructor. As you consider the following questions, you will need to take several steps away from your writing and pretend you are a *reader* rather than the writer. (It takes some practice to effectively look at your own writing from the stance of a reader, but it is well worth the effort.)

Many of the items on this checklist have been specifically covered as you have worked your way through this book. Others are items that readers often look for, consciously or unconsciously.

- ☐ **Focus.** Will a reader know what your topic is and what point you want to make about it?
- ☐ **Appropriate detail.** Are all aspects of the paper clearly tied to the topic and point?
- ☐ **Adequate detail.** Has the reader been given enough examples, reasons, etc. to clearly understand the point being focused on?
- ☐ **Structure.** Can the reader identify and follow a logical organization of details?
- ☐ **Significance.** Is the importance of the experience made clear to the reader?
- ☐ **Reflection.** Does the writer examine his or her experience and draw conclusions?
- ☐ **Personal voice.** Does the writer communicate in a natural-sounding manner, avoiding stilted, overly formal expression?

Read through one of your possible portfolio selections and reconsider your draft in the light of the above two approaches. Even at this stage do not be afraid to make major changes in your paper as you think about the needs of your reader.

READING FOR CORRECTNESS

You can work a long time on a paper and do a great job with focus and development, but if there are errors in grammar and punctuation, readers may take a dim view of all your hard work. Attending to correctness is the important final stage before submitting your portfolio.

The following exercises are designed to give you practice in identifying and correcting errors that a reader may find distracting.

Recognizing Sentence Boundaries

The following student-written stories have been altered to give you practice finding sentence boundaries. There is no punctuation to signal the end of a sentence, and there is no capitalization to show where a new sentence begins.

1. Read each story aloud. Notice how the lack of end punctuation and capitalization makes it difficult to read.
2. Alone, with a partner, or in a group, rewrite the stories by adding a period at the end of each sentence and a capital letter at the beginning of each sentence.
3. Read your corrected version aloud, making sure that your sentences are complete.

```
       The Rocket and the Pellet Gun


It was one of those hot summer days in the late
seventies, and I was about thirteen or fourteen
years old I was in my back yard shooting beer
cans with my 760 Crossman pellet gun, pretending
I was a crack shot competing with other marks-
men for the Olympic gold I was pumping the pel-
let gun to full pressure and loading as fast as
I could, trying to hit the cans that I had
lined up as many times as I could.
   I was sighting in on my target when I heard
the distinct sound of a model rocket going off,
with its hissing sound that the rocket engines
make I immediately stopped what I was doing and
stared upward, facing a deep blue, cloudless sky
I saw the trail of white smoke and a small mis-
sile hurling through the sky. I stared at the
```

rocket until it was almost out of sight then a fluorescent orange colored parachute popped out from the fuselage the parachute started to unravel, and it opened up the rocket was returning back to earth.

The rocket had been launched from across the street where John Harris lived I knew it must have been he who launched the rocket because we would sometimes build and launch rockets together John Harris was about three or four years older than I was because of our neighborly relationship, we became acquaintances.

I walked across the road to his house to see if he was going to launch any more rockets as I did, I could see him in the field, running after his rocket that the wind was carrying high above the open field when I arrived at the launching pad, John Smoot was there also he's my other neighbor who was a year older than John Harris after John Smoot and I said our greetings, we turned and saw John Harris returning with his rocket in hand John Harris wrapped the parachute up and stuffed it back in the top part of the fuselage and replaced the cone he removed the used fuel cell and place a new one in its position John Harris was preparing the rocket for another launch.

As I stood next to Smoot, Harris slipped the rocket through the wire guide and hooked up the electric connectors that would ignite the fuel cell Harris started the count down, beginning with ten, and counted backwards this was just a backyard launch but he took it as seriously as if NASA were launching one of its rockets toward outer space Harris was finishing the countdown—three, two, one, take off, and hit the button to ignite the rocket engine in an instant, the rocket took off the launch pad and darted through the endless sky, making a noise like a blow torch and leaving a cloud of light blue smoke where it once had been the rocket zoomed skyward until it was just a visible dot we all watched the rocket carefully so we would know where it went in case the wind carried it away we waited for gravity to take hold of the rocket and pull it back to earth.

The rocket's orange parachute opened up and was gliding back to earth when a gust of wind grabbed hold and carried the rocket toward the tree line where it snagged on the branches of a huge old oak tree we all headed to the tree where the rocket had unfortunately landed I was still carrying the pellet gun all this time Harris asked me if I would climb up the tree to get his rocket for him it was known that Harris was scared of heights, and he did not have the agility to climb trees I told him it was no problem but I would need a boost up to reach the branches Harris clasped his hands together, and I put my left foot in his clasped hands while he heaved me up I grabbed hold of the branch and started to shimmy up the tree the rocket wasn't that high up, and I would have retrieved it with no difficulty.

I climbed through the intertwine of branches, getting closer to the rocket I could hear and see Harris shooting my pellet gun as he waited down below I was just in reach of his rocket when I felt a sharp stinging sensation coming from my right butt cheek feeling as though I was stung by a hornet, my concentration was greatly distracted my first concern was what had happened I looked below, seeing Harris grinning behind my rifle, realizing he shot me with my own gun I said a few choice words for I wasn't happy about what he had just done, especially when I was doing him a favor by climbing the tree to retrieve his rocket he thought what he had done was funny but I wasn't laughing with him I was angry at what he had just done I left the rocket where it was and started down the tree, saying to heck with his rocket I wanted to get even the thought then occurred that he might try shooting me again while I was in the tree so I moved quickly down, so as not to give him another chance to shoot me when I was just about to jump out of the tree.

In the months that followed, John Harris and I launched our model rockets off together but I always left my pellet gun at home I separated my two hobbies so that another incident such as that one wouldn't happen again.

Tribute to Pawee

I came home from high school with my girl-friend, thinking only about the upcoming basketball game that night we walked in the door, laughing about something that had happened on the way home from school when I saw my mother and father crying I was in shock I didn't know what had happened they said, "Pawee died." Pawee was my grandfather I stood there as if nothing had happened after they left to go to the hospital to fill out some papers, my girlfriend called her parents to pick her up, and I got a roast beef sandwich to eat I stood in the kitchen and stared out of the window for about ten minutes.

Later that night it still hadn't really set in because my mind was only on my basketball, but I played really well that night I could feel Pawee looking over me as I scored twenty-six points against Edison South in a varsity game.

When I got home that night, I went upstairs and lay in bed thinking about Pawee I started to cry because I already missed him and I wanted him back then I started thinking about it he was now with my grandmother, who was already in heaven she passed away two years before he did he was lonely and in pain those last two years I think that was what had killed him.

He was the kind of man that would do anything for you he was a strict but kind man he liked watching football and basketball, especially watching my junior high games I made him proud, but he never pushed me to play these sports.

When I was a young boy, Pawee, my brother Coy, and I would go out to get ice cream every Saturday he would also buy my little brother and me those battery operated cars that we could drive he really spoiled us even though he

was not a wealthy man my grandfather taught my
brother and me to cuss he thought it was really
funny that little kids were saying cuss words
as Coy and I grew older, Pawee would tell us to
fight for things we believed in and also taught
us other things that would come in handy in the
future I will never forget all the memories I
have of him.

At his funeral I kept myself from breaking
down in front of all of our friends and family
I stood around and people kept hugging me and
asking me how I was doing my mother was amazed
that I wasn't crying I was hurting on the
inside though.

It has been two years now, and I think about
him often I miss his smile and great sense of
humor I will always remember him if you're listening to me, Pawee, I love you.

Correcting Comma Splices

The purpose of punctuation is to help the reader. When two sentences
are joined incorrectly, a reader must often *reread* the sentence in order
to understand the writer's message.

The following student-written essays have been altered to give you
practice catching and correcting sentences that have been connected
incorrectly. Work alone, with a partner, or in a group as you rewrite
the essays to make them easier to read.

When two complete sentences are joined by only a comma, we call
the result a *comma splice*. You may correct a comma splice in a number of ways.

- Consider separating the two sentences with a period.
- Perhaps insert a coordinating conjunction after the comma to
  show the relationship between the two sentences. (Coordinating
  conjunctions: and but or for so yet nor)

- If the two sentences are closely related, you may wish to replace the comma with a semicolon instead of a period.
- Think carefully about the relationship between the two sentences. A transitional word after a semicolon can emphasize the relationship between the sentences. (There is a list of transitional words at the end of this book.)
- You may feel that the two parts of your comma splice would work better if you completely rewrote the sentences.

```
         Feeling Like an Outsider


When I attended Thornton Junior High School in
the 1970's, I was real skinny, therefore, I
felt like an outsider. I was thirteen years old
and wearing a size one, whenever a big gust of
wind came, it nearly knocked me down. People
often teased me and called me names like Olive
Oyle, Wilma, or Skinny Minny. Whenever we had
gym, I was scared to show my body because it
was so bony and I knew people would laugh, when
they laughed, I felt like an outsider. It wasn't
until my freshman year when I joined the track
team that my classmates realized there was more
to my skinny body than just something to laugh
at. The coach convinced me that with such a
small frame I should try running, therefore, I
joined the track team and became one of their
fastest runners. I set various records in the
relay, high jump, and mile run, by the time I
left that school, I was voted most popular and
had received many plaques and trophies. I will
never forget Coach Malone, I often thank him
silently for the self-confidence he gave me.
That part of my life is over, I'm all grown up,
and whenever I see a skinny person, I go out of
```

my way to pay him or her a compliment, just in case that person, too, has been humiliated because of his or her size.

Desert Shield/Storm

Upon joining the Armed Forces of the United States of America, I always wondered if I would ever have to go to war. NAH! As I was proudly sworn in as a Marine Corps recruit, I thought, "This will never happen to me, I'll just do my duty and get out." Well, that wasn't the case, like my father, I was sent to war at a very young age, however, my father was sent to Vietnam and I (twenty some years later) was sent to the Persian Gulf for Operation Desert Shield/Storm. One officer, forty-one enlisted men, and I were activated from the Marine Corps Reserve to active duty. I, along with my colleagues, had never done anything like this before, we had been through many combat training exercises, but this was to be the real thing.

We left on December 10, 1990, for an unpleasant thirty-hour plane trip on board an American Airlines 747 jumbo jet, when we arrived in Saudi Arabia, we were all very pessimistic about what was going to happen to us. Since our job was the processing of human remains, we were worried that we would catch some kind of disease, fortunately, that did not happen.

Time passed, and the war started, I knew I would have to do my job, Grave Registration. This is where two soldiers, when given a casualty of war, process the human remains and send the deceased back to the rear for staging, processing includes fingerprinting, recording of personal and military effects, and notation of all visible physical injuries.

I had never seen anyone die before my eyes, I had certainly never seen deceased bodies lying around on gurneys, awaiting their turn to be processed. I had never seen what a bullet or a piece of shrapnel could do to a human skull, I knew nothing about what someone looks like after diving on a grenade to save his buddy's life. I couldn't have imagined what an eighteen-year-old kid looks like after floating face down in The Gulf for a week, I was appalled by the malodorous smell that a deceased, decaying body gives off WAR STINKS!

Weeks went by, I had processed many remains. As I processed them, I wondered what their parents were thinking, what they were saying to each other, and how they would react if they knew what I was doing at that exact moment in time. They were probably thinking, "Ah Nothing's gonna happen to my son, he'll be home soon." Unfortunately, there were many cases where this was not true.

After the war ended, we were sent back to the rear to gather up some things and be on our way home, this gave me a little time to look back and recap all I had done in the four and one half months that I was there, I realized that I learned three valuable things. They are always be thankful for who you are, for what you have, and for the free country in which you live.

Finding and Correcting Run-Ons

Readers have trouble when writers run two sentences together with no punctuation between them. When two sentences have no conjunction or punctuation between them, we often call the result a *run-on sentence.*

The following student-written essays have been altered to give you practice finding and correcting sentences that have been run together. Work alone, with a partner, or in a group as you rewrite the essays to make them easier to read.

If you find two sentences run together, you may correct the run-on in a number of ways:

- Separate the two sentences with end punctuation (period, question mark, exclamation point).
- Combine the sentences, using an appropriate coordinating conjunction with proper punctuation.
- If the two sentences are closely related, you may wish to combine them by using a semicolon with or without a transitional word.
- You may feel that the two sentences would sound better if you completely rewrote them.

```
                Learning to Write


I started writing at the age of four writing
was very hard for me at first I never could
figure out a comfortable method of holding my
pencil it did not matter if it was skinny or
fat. I would always hold my pencil too tight
for fear that I would drop it. My hands shook
every time I wrote anything I was very nervous
about not doing it the correct way it looked
like chicken scratch. My parents were always
very supportive of me they would tell me the
truth about how good or bad my writing was. Mom
would sit down next to me when she had some
spare time and guide me in writing my numbers
```

and capital as well as lower case letters. Letters and numbers had lots of lines and curves to learn if I had a problem making any particular one, Mom would make them and have me trace them with tracing paper over and over again until I did them the correct way.

My lines were sometimes straight and at other times crooked my letters were upside down or right side up. My numbers were forward and backward I guess I was confused there were a lot of them to learn. If my pencil would break, I would get very frustrated and cry if my pencils were not sharp enough and did not have a clean eraser, I did not want to use them anymore they made my papers smudgy and very messy. I sometimes would go and throw my pencils straight into the nearest trash can. Then I would grab a new one I was glad I was able to throw my old pencils away Mom made sure I had plenty of them. Sometimes Mom would give me a funny look she was not angry with me because she knew that was the way I was about my old, broken, and dirty pencils.

Although I hadn't started kindergarten, I had a vivid memory of always wanting to do my best in writing because my parents stressed how important good handwriting skills were. Later on in life, I appreciated having learned these skills that have helped me so much in high school, college, and on my job as a medical secretary. Now as a mother, I have continued to pass on these writing skills to my three school age children in hopes that this will help them

in life as it has helped me I have bought
plenty of pencils, paper, pens, and a good pencil sharpener because my kids are a lot like me
when I was growing up. Hopefully, they will
pass on this tradition of good handwriting
skills to their children as I have.

A Lovers' Quarrel

When I was a child, the two most exciting people
in my life were my parents. There was always
something happening around the house it seemed
more like a scene from a movie than real life.
  There is one memory that I am particularly
fond of because it was so comical. It was a
beautiful spring night my mother and father were
having a "lovers' spat." He wanted to spend an
evening at the race tracks without my mother
she was bent on going with him. He was in the
shower preparing for the night ahead she sneaked
outside to the car and let the air out of all
four of his tires. She returned to the living
room feeling very smug and believing that she
had ousted him out of his night on the town. My
father came out of the bedroom smartly dressed
and ready for the race tracks he slipped my
mother a kiss and headed out the door. She simply smiled slyly she wished him a nice time. My
father walked down the driveway my mother softly
laughed behind his back. A short amount of time
passed I heard him yell for her. She strolled
down the driveway she had a satisfied spring in
her step. I silently followed her, anxiously
waiting to see what would happen next.

My father had gotten the tire pump for our
bikes out of the backyard he held it out to
her. The only words he uttered were, "Start
pumping," as she took the pump from him. So
there was my mother, crestfallen, standing
beside the car going up and down, over and over
again, she pumped air back into each of the
tires. My father just sat quietly on the front
steps with the same smug look my mother was
wearing only a few minutes ago. Two hours later
she finished the last tire we both looked at my
father and awaited his next move. He slowly got
to his feet, passed both us and the car, and
went over to his motorcycle. He got on, started
it up, and then left my mother standing there,
gaping! My mother was so infuriated she wasn't
about to let him have the last word.

She ran into the house she fixed her make-up
she ran back out. She started down the street,
muttering that she was definitely not going to
sit at home! We, my sisters and I, were all on
the porch watching her leave we heard dad's
motorcycle come around the corner. It seemed
that he had expected her to do something like
this he had gone around the block and watched
from around the corner. He drove down the
street after her he even ran the bike up onto
the sidewalk to block her path until she gave
in and came back home. So there was mom, out-
smarted again, but too tired to do anything
about it. We all went into the house after her,
wishing we could help, but not knowing how.

A few hours later, after everything had set-
tled down, we heard my father's bike pull into

the driveway. My mother jumped up with excitement, hoping that he had come back to get her. He walked into the house noticeably agitated about something he told my mother to get dressed so that she could leave with him. He explained that a woman at the bar had called him a "dirty biker" and that he wanted my mother to kick her butt if she didn't apologize.

It was not long after they left that my mother was once again home, and furious! The fight was over my mother came out victorious my father dropped her off back at home. She was so frustrated and angry that she decided that she was going to have the last laugh—no matter what! So she went outside into the yard and picked up a nearby brick. She walked with determination up to the front of the car and heaved the brick through the windshield with all her might the brick put a large hole in the windshield that my mother seemed very proud of. She walked back into the house with a smile on her face and with the knowledge that she had truly gotten the last laugh in her heart.

The last words that she spoke that evening were, "All things considered, I guess it hasn't been too bad of a night," and I had to agree with her!

Adding Appropriate Internal Punctuation

Once again—the purpose of punctuation is to help the reader understand what the writer is trying to say. Although end punctuation (the kind that separates sentences) is vital to a reader's understanding, internal punctuation (within a sentence) can be equally important. If a sentence is properly punctuated, a reader is more likely to understand it the *first* time that he or she reads it.

The following student-written essays have been altered to give you practice adding internal punctuation. The end punctuation that appears is correct. Your job is to find places to add commas *within* the sentences.

Some of the ways that you have practiced using internal punctuation are as follows:

- To separate an introductory subordinate clause from the rest of the sentence.
- To separate items in a series.
- To appropriately separate two or more adjectives that appear immediately before the noun that they describe.
- To separate introductory adverbs from the sentence.
- To separate introductory prepositional phrases from the sentence.
- To separate nonessential relative clauses from the rest of the sentence. (Relative clauses that begin with *who* or *which* and are *not needed to identify* the noun they follow.)
- To separate appositives from the rest of the sentence.
- To separate participial phrases from the rest of the sentence when appropriate.

```
              Uncle Harvey


The one man who has been an influence on me has
been my uncle Harvey Riles. My Uncle Harvey is
a thirty-two year old man about six feet and
three inches tall. He weighs around two hundred
and thirty pounds is bald and has very dark
skin thick eyebrows and brown eyes. When Harvey
talks you can see his face muscles bulge.
Harvey who is a member of the Alpha fraternity
has an Alpha brand of the letter A on his right
arm. He has big hands, and on the bottom they
are pink and chapped from the work he does for
the city. When he walks he has a distinctive
limp because he blew his knee out playing foot-
ball when he was little.
```

Harvey is sometimes very loud and enthusiastic when he comes to visit. He loves to talk about anything at all and sometimes gets crazy when we go out to parties. He is very competitive in basketball football and his work, for he always wants to be the best at what he does.

My uncle and I are both Hoban High School alums; therefore, I want to follow in his footsteps. Uncle Harvey was the first man in our family to attend college Kent State University. Harvey would sometimes invite me up to the university to experience college life. I was always enthusiastic about hanging around the older guys and experiencing the college life, but it was Harvey's success in college that motivated me to go and do as well as he did. During my uncle's five years of college he accumulated a grade point average of over a three point and was the best art major in his field.

My Uncle Harvey is to me like a best friend not only an uncle. He also poses as a father figure to me because he has been the only man in my life since my mother and father got a divorce. He has always been there for me during the good times and the bad times. Harvey has been there for me when I was struggling in my grades gave me support and helped me study. He was at sporting events celebrating my accomplishments. Harvey is someone I know I can always come and talk to. He is my role model because I like the qualities that he possesses such as his determination his good attitude and his creativity. I hope some day I will possess those qualities.

A Child Deals With Death

Death is an experience that we all feel pretty confused about. When one of our loved ones dies it is very hard to deal with. Such was the case when my grandfather died.

My grandfather was a very good man. He was a short darkhaired strong full blooded Italian. My grandpa had a very large family eight children and eighteen grandchildren. Whenever anyone visited him he would be very generous to his company. He regularly fed his grandchildren cookies pop and candy. Although he was cruel and mean to is own children he always treated his grandchildren with respect. I was his youngest grandchild and was always very special to him. I really enjoyed his company when I went to see him, for we used to play with his dog Heidi together. And I felt really special when he called me by the nickname that he gave me "Nicola."

When I was about ten years old he started becoming very ill. Sugar diabetes a bad liver and very bad circulation were among his troubles. My grandfather a stubborn man was in and out of the hospital many times, but he never listened to the doctors or nurses. One day he had so bad of a stroke that he went into a coma for a week. When I went to see him while he was in the coma I felt sad depressed and very hurt. I could not stand to see my grandpa in a position like that. After he woke up he was a totally different man. He could not remember who anyone was, and my family was forced to place him in a nursing home.

Every time I went to see him sadness came upon me. Although I tried to talk to him he did not even know who I was. One night before I went to sleep my dad came into my bedroom and told me that my grandfather had passed away. I felt such a shock that I started crying and ran downstairs to talk with my mother. She told me that my grandfather had been going through a great deal of pain, and passing away would be the best thing for him. After I talked with her I felt much better.

Death is something that hurts all of us. When someone we care about is not going to be with us anymore it leaves us feeling lonely. But sometimes it can be the best thing. My grandfather has no more pain and is very well and happy in heaven. He will always have a special place in my heart.

A Great Relationship

The relationship between my mother and me is very tight. We both love trust and respect each other. I love her and care about anything she thinks. I've lived eighteen years, and most of it was spent with my loving mother.

My mother who is a successful service representative for the telephone company with twenty-two years service is the best mom I could ever have. I was born in Cleveland when she was twenty-two, and she has given me food a roof and love which made me feel loved as a kid. Growing up with my mom was always fun because she would take time to take me on outings and

to attend the baseball games that I would play.
When I got older she kept me out of trouble and
in school.

She has let me do things on my own which made
me an independent person, and she backs me up in
almost everything I do. Most of the time she's
cool and laid back; however, on occasion she can
get upset and lecture me on something, but it's
usually for the best. We basically have a good
mother-son relationship, for we look out for
each other which shows our protective bond.

My mom's approval is very important to me.
Although I now make all my decisions myself my
mother is still there for me. If she approves
of the things I do then our relationship is
even better. Although I am now a grown man when
I am around my mom I feel like a kid. And it
feels just fine.

Samantha

Kathy my fiancée and I got a dog earlier this
year. Samantha a black Lab and Newfoundland mix
breed gives us plenty of love and companionship;
moreover, she gives Kathy a sense of protection
while I am at work which is mostly in the
evenings.

When I come home from work Samantha is always
sitting at the door waiting for me to come in.
As I look in the door she starts wagging her
tail furiously her ears lay back and her body
starts shaking ready to explode at me with an
abundance of love and happiness. When I open the
door Sam rushes to me kissing my hands and rub-

bing her shiny soft black coat against me. This
is Sam's way of expressing her love for me and
her joy that I am home. Coming home to such a
display of affection can make my worst day seem
like a thing of the past totally forgotten. After
we have said our hellos to each other Sam wants
to play. She grabs one of her many toys and
brings it to me. If she brings me her ball we
play catch for a while. Sometimes she will bring
me her towel, and she wants to play tug-o-war. I
think she does this to show me how strong and
tough she is, and that she is quite capable of
protecting us if she needed to.

One night after dinner Kathy was finishing
cleaning up the kitchen, and Sam was by her
side. I was downstairs and decided to put on my
bald-headed old man rubber Halloween mask to see
what Sam would do. I started up the stairs, and
she curiously came to see who was coming. When
she saw an unfamiliar face coming at her she
started barking viciously, and the hair on her
back stood up instantly. She continued barking
and growling keeping herself between me and
Kathy. The closer I came to them the more she
barked and growled. When Sam thought that this
strange man me was too close to her and Kathy
she lunged and snapped her teeth at me. I
called her name as I took off the mask. The
familiar face along with the recognized voice
put her at ease. She had to smell me to make
certain it was really me. She then gave me this
look like, "If you ever do that again I will
bit you in the a___!" I was happy to see Sam was

ready to protect Kathy by putting herself between Kathy and danger. This in my view is the strongest way of demonstrating her love and devotion to us.

Kathy and I love Sam very much. We jokingly call her our daughter, and in fact she is an important part of our family like any child would be. I would not trade her for anything in the world.

Additional Practice

SENTENCE COMBINING REVIEWS

Sentence Combining Practice

Use all the techniques that you have learned as you combine the following groups of sentences. You can make correct sentences in a number of ways. Try combining each group in several different ways. Do some work better than others?

Sentence Review #1: A Memorable Experience

1. One summer about five years ago, I made plans to go to Mohican State Park.

   A few of my friends made plans to go to Mohican State Park.

   The plans were to go canoeing.

   _____

   _____

2. It was a sunny day.

   It was a beautiful day, considering that it had just rained a few days before.

The river was swollen.

_____

_____

_____

3. We knew it would be a little risky.
   The currents were moving quickly.
   The currents were very strong.
   We decided to go anyway.
   We had been planning this for a month.

_____

_____

4. We got two canoes.
   We started on our journey.
   The journey was for five miles.
   The journey was down the river.

_____

_____

_____

5. We traveled down the river awhile.
   We decided to use our life vests.
   We used the vests to tie the canoes together.
   We decided to drift down the river.

_____

_____

_____

6. We were all pretty good swimmers.
   We didn't think we needed them.

_____

_____

7. This happened about half way through our
   journey.
   We came to a tree.
   The tree had been blown over by the storm.
   The roots were sticking up right in front of
   us in the water.

   _____

   _____

   _____

8. The current pushed us sideways.
   The current pushed us right into the roots.

   _____

   _____

9. We decided to just sit there for a while.
   We decided to watch all the debris wash down
   the river.
   Another canoe with a family was headed right
   for us.
   The family had a husband and wife.
   The family had two small children.

   _____

   _____

   _____

10. They tried to stay away from us.
    The current was too strong.
    It pushed them right up against us.

    _____

    _____

    _____

11. The man moved too quickly.

He flipped over the canoe.

_____

_____

12. We didn't panic at first.
    They were all wearing life vests.
    We thought they would surface.

_____

_____

13. The man and the woman surfaced.
    They surfaced rapidly.
    It happened so fast.
    They didn't grab the two small children.

_____

_____

_____

14. The woman realized the children didn't
    surface.
    She started screaming about her babies.

_____

_____

15. We jumped out of our canoes into the four
    feet of water.
    We jumped out quickly.
    We were not even thinking we were not wearing
    our life vests.

_____

_____

_____

16. We were reaching under the canoe.
    We were thinking they might be trapped against the tree roots.

    _____

    _____

17. I felt something brush by me.
    I couldn't grasp it.

    _____

    _____

18. One of my friends found the four-year-old.
    The four-year-old was against the tree roots.
    He pulled her up.
    He pulled quickly.
    She started to cry.
    She cried immediately.

    _____

    _____

    _____

19. We were relieved she was okay.
    The mother was screaming about her baby being gone.
    There was no sign of the other child.

    _____

    _____

    _____

20. We were all spread out.
    We were all searching frantically.
    We were not finding anything.
    My friend Mike spotted an orange life vest.

---

21. He moved as fast as he could.
    He moved through the high currents.
    The currents were fast moving.

---

22. He got to the life vest.
    He found a small body within the vest.
    The body was small.
    The body was water-logged.
    The body was lifeless.

---

23. He dragged the little girl to the side of the
    river bank.
    He had to start CPR on the child.
    He had to start immediately.
    The child was three years old.

---

24. The child did finally respond.
    She started choking.
    She started crying.

_____

_____

25. The parents were so happy.
    I felt so relieved.
    I started to cry.

_____

_____

26. The parents got back into the canoe.
    The children got back into the canoe.
    They thanked us more than enough.

_____

_____

27. We finished our journey.
    We were dumbfounded by what had happened.

_____

_____

28. Saving these children was one of the events
    of my life.
    The event was most overwhelming.
    The event was joyous.

_____

_____

29. I was just thankful that they lived.
    I can't imagine how I could have dealt with
    this if they had not survived.

_____

_____

Sentence Review #2: Imagining

1. On rainy days we played.
   My siblings and I played.
   We played in our bedroom the whole day.

   _____

   _____

2. We used a yellow pop-up toy.
   The toy was for the steering wheel.
   The steering wheel was for our bed car.

   _____

   _____

3. We traveled all over the country.
   We traveled in our car.
   At times we went around the world.

   _____

   _____

4. Our favorite place to visit was Mexico.
   My sister and I had just finished reading the
   book *Mexicali Soup*.

   _____

   _____

5. We went to the grocery store.
   The grocery store was in Mexico.
   We went to buy the special ingredients.
   The ingredients were for the soup.

   _____

   _____

6. We would get out of our car.
   We would walk around the room.

We were picking up toys.
We were pretending to get the ingredients.

_____

_____

7. We purchased the items.
   We got back in the car.
   We started to drive back to the States.

_____

_____

8. We drove back to the States.
   We stopped at Hollywood.

_____

_____

9. We were a famous singing group.
   We were in Hollywood.

_____

_____

10. We would put on fancy clothes.
    We would have a concert.
    We would give out autographs after the
    concert.

_____

_____

11. We left Hollywood.
    It was time for us to eat.
    We would go to McDonald's.

_____

_____

12. We pretended to go to McDonald's.

We would put on a coat that my mom always wore.

She wore it when we went through the drive thru.

_____

_____

13. We wore the coat.

It made a noise when we would roll down our pretend window.

It was the same noise it would make when my mom wore it to McDonald's.

_____

_____

14. We didn't want to go to McDonald's.

We went to our favorite five-star restaurant.

The restaurant was our dining room.

_____

_____

15. We were at the restaurant.

We would order gourmet peanut butter and jelly sandwiches.

_____

_____

16. We would wash it down with a glass of milk.

We would wash it down leisurely.

The glass was large.

The milk was cold.

_____

_____

17. After our lunch, we would go to the bathroom.
    After our lunch, we would get back on the
    road.

    _____

    _____

18. We drove for hours.
    It was time for our nap.

    _____

    _____

19. We would sleep for a few hours.
    We would continue our journey.

    _____

    _____

20. We went to Disneyland.
    We would talk to the characters in our
    imaginary world.
    We would walk around the park.
    We were going to the shows.
    We were riding the rides.

    _____

    _____

    _____

21. We would purchase items.
    The items were for our parents.
    The items were souvenirs.

    _____

    _____

22. We would continue to play at Disneyland.

We played for a few more hours.
We would get on the road to go home.

_____

_____

23. We arrived back at home.
    We parked our car.
    We got out.
    We went into the living room.
    We went to watch our favorite television shows.
    Our favorites were *The Flintstones* and *Scooby-Doo*.

_____

_____

_____

24. We watched our cartoons.
    We would still use our imaginations.
    We would pretend that we were at the movies.

_____

_____

_____

25. We ate dinner later.
    We would tell our parents about our great journey.
    We would tell them what we bought them at Disneyland.

_____

_____

_____

26. The day came to an end.
    We took our baths.
    We went to bed.

    _____

    _____

27. We woke up the next morning.
    We woke up with much anticipation.
    We were ready to take on the next adventure.
    It might rain.
    It might shine.

    _____

    _____

Combining Sentences in a Paragraph

As you rewrite the following student-written paragraphs, make them
sound more sophisticated by combining sentences. You can combine
the sentences correctly in a number of ways. Change the paragraphs
so that they sound good to *you*.

Paragraph #1: The Burn

When I was about five years old, I had a very
painful experience. I can still remember it as
clear as day. It was a clear mid-September
afternoon. My mother decided to fix me some
lunch. I told her I wanted some chicken noodle
soup. While she was putting the water on the
stove to boil I decided to get the crackers and
my soup mug out. I was extremely hungry, and I
was eating very fast. I decided that I needed
some more crackers for my soup. Quickly, I
reached over for the crackers. As I was doing
that, I bumped my soup mug over. Boiling hot

soup ran all down my legs and stomach. I felt
so scared and petrified. I yelled OUCH! ! ! !,
and started screaming continuously. I yelled for
my mother to come. She came running up our
basement steps. "What's Wrong?" she cried. I
just stood there in hysterics with hot boiling
soup running down my body. I was feeling a
tremendous amount of pain. She picked me up,
and ran me upstairs to the bathroom. She threw
me in the bathtub of ice cold water. I never
felt so scared, terrified, and hurt in my life.
While my mother was pouring cold water on me, I
was crying at the top of my lungs. My burn was
so bad, skin was falling off my stomach. My
whole stomach looked like it was falling off. A
week later, a huge scab appeared on my stomach.
My mother decided to take me to my family doctor. On the way to the doctor, I was very nervous and scared. I did not know what to expect
when I got to the doctor. When we got to the
doctor's office, the doctor looked at my burn.
He told my mother and me that it was a very bad
abrasion. He said it was a second degree burn.
The doctor told my mother that she did the
right thing by putting me in ice cold water.
Before we left his office, he gave me cream to
put on my burn. It took about two months for
the large scab to disappear from my stomach.

I can still remember that terrible day very
well. I will never be able to forget about such
a terrifying experience. To this day the scar
still appears on my stomach. Whenever I look at

it, it reminds me of that awful time. I will
never be able to forget it because the scar will
probably remain there for the rest of my life.

Paragraph #2: Wonder Woman

There are special people in my life that I look
up to. I admire them. They are my mother, grandmother, aunts, uncles, and cousins. However,
none of them had that so-called "hero impact" on
me. There was one person who did. That person
was WONDER WOMAN. I don't know exactly what it
was about her that made me want to be just like
her. Maybe it was that she was one of the first
female superheroes. Or maybe it was because she
could catch all the bad guys. She caught them
with her lasso. She didn't need any super
vision. She didn't need any super hearing. She
didn't need any super flying powers like
Superman had.

She stood about 5 feet 7 1/2 inches tall. She
wore a crown on her head. She wore a halter-top
shirt. She wore blue shorts and red high heeled
boots. She had bracelets that could stop bul-
lets. She had a lasso on her hip. She also had
the power of making you think about the wrong
that you were doing and making you do the right
thing. She had an invisible plane that she used
to fight her crimes in. To me she was the best
superhero there was. Not SUPERMAN or BATMAN and
ROBIN, WONDER WOMAN she was the best. She cap-
tured the bad guys by herself. She even came to

the rescue of SUPERMAN and BATMAN at times. One moment she would be her normal self. She was just another person walking down the street. Then she would get this feeling that a crime was taking place somewhere. She would find a place where there were no people around. She would go behind something. She would come out. She would do three spins. Then she would be "WONDER WOMAN." She would be off to fight crime and to catch the bad guys.

She had her own T.V. show that starred Linda Carter. The show came on every afternoon Monday through Friday. I had to watch it every day that it came on. I didn't even know how to tell time. When it was time for WONDER WOMAN to come on, I would be sitting in front of the T.V. waiting. Every time WONDER WOMAN was changing into her WONDER WOMAN outfit, I would be in front of the T.V. I would be doing my three spins just like her. I was wishing that I too could change into WONDER WOMAN. I don't know exactly what it was that made me love WONDER WOMAN and want to be just like her. Maybe it was because when I was growing up, I was told that a girl wasn't supposed to do this. Girls could not do the same things as boys. But WONDER WOMAN was a girl too. She could do anything she wanted to. She could do the same things boys did if not better.

I guess that's why I had WONDER WOMAN stickers. I had T-shirts. I had pajamas, undershirts, and underwear. You name it; I had it. I was even WONDER WOMAN for Halloween in kindergarten. I still have that costume to this day. Not only was WONDER WOMAN a superhero, but she was also a woman. She could do anything. I guess that's why I wanted to be so much like her. Wonder Woman—she was the best!

Appendixes

COORDINATION

Using Coordinating Conjunctions

1. When you connect *two complete sentences* with a *coordinating conjunction,* a comma is often used before the conjunction.

    ,and—shows a simple connection between sentences

    ,or—shows a choice between sentences

    ,for—connects sentences only when it means *because*

    ,but—shows a contrast between sentences

    ,so—connects sentences only when it means *as a result*

    ,yet—means *but*

2. *Do not* use a comma before the conjunction when you connect *parts* of sentences.

    College students can discover ways to balance their studies *and* their social lives.
       I can sign up for math tutoring on Mondays *or* Tuesdays.

Using Semicolons to Join Complete Sentences

1. When two sentences are joined by a *semicolon,* the second sentence explains, comments on, or gives details about the first sentence.

    > I want to improve my writing ability; I am taking Basic Writing to refresh my skills.
    >   College Reading helps students improve their vocabulary skills; it also teaches them how to read their textbooks more effectively.
    >   Sometimes I can focus my freewriting easily; on other occasions I change my mind several times before deciding on a focus.

    - There is a complete sentence on each side of the semicolon.
    - The relationship between the sentences is relatively clear to a reader.
    - The word that appears after the semicolon is not capitalized.

2. *Transitional words* and phrases can be used after a semicolon to connect two sentences. When they are used this way, they are followed by commas.

; therefore,		
;consequently,	means *as a result*	
; thus,		

;then,	show a time	
;finally,	relationship	

;however,		
;nevertheless,	mean *but*	

;furthermore,	means *and*	

SUBORDINATION

1. Dependent clauses often begin with *subordinating conjunctions.* Here is a partial list.

after	as though	so (meaning *so that*)	until
although	because	so that	when
as	before	than	whenever
as if	even if	that	where
as long as	if	though	wherever
as soon as	since	unless	while

    - Use a comma after a dependent clause that begins a sentence.
    - A dependent clause that appears at the end of a sentence does not require a comma.

Because college students deserve help with their writing, the University provides free tutoring in the Writing Lab.

Whenever you have writer's block, try making yourself freewrite for ten minutes.

You may find yourself actually enjoying writing *if you consult with a tutor regularly*.

2. A *Relative clause* is used as an adjective and normally follows the noun that it modifies. Relative clauses usually begin with a relative pronoun. Here are some common relative pronouns:

that   who   whom   which   whose

- Use commas to separate the relative clause from the rest of the sentence when the clause is not necessary to *identify* the noun being described.
- Do not separate the relative clause from the rest of the sentence when the clause is *necessary* to identify the noun.

The person *who taught Rodney how to use a computer* is now a millionaire.

Professor Redmond, *who taught Rodney how to use a computer*, is now a millionaire.

DETAILS AND DESCRIPTION

1. Writers often use a *series* of nouns, verbs, or descriptive elements to avoid repetition.

When I make pizza, I like to add *pepperoni, mushrooms, onions, peppers, and sausage.* [Series of nouns]

I have learned how to *mix, toss, and bake* perfect pizza dough.
[Series of verbs]

Mr. Montoni's pizza is always *fresh, hot, and juicy.* [Series of adjectives]

Mr. Montoni prides himself in *using fresh ingredients, being generous with toppings, and serving piping-hot pizzas.* [Series of phrases]

- Separate each item in the series from the others by using a comma.

- Include a comma before the *and* that introduces the last item.
- Read aloud to help you determine whether all items in your series are balanced.

2. When two or more *adjectives* appear *immediately before a noun*, use a comma to separate the adjectives when it might also make sense to use the word *and* instead of the comma.

   I like a rich, brown crust on fried chicken.

   I like a rich, crisp, brown crust on fried chicken.

3. When an *adverb* is used as an introductory word, a comma is placed after it. Otherwise, adverbs usually require no special punctuation.

   Carefully, Emil places the condiments on his *enormously* thick pizza.

4. *Prepositional phrases* require no special punctuation unless they begin a sentence.

   After a long drought, the clown and I escaped *from prison on a flying carpet*.

5. Like some relative clauses, *appositives* that are not needed to identify the noun they rename are set off from the rest of the sentence by a comma or by a set of commas.

   Chicken, *my favorite food*, is good for me.

   Many people also love Joe's favorite food, *tacos*.

6. *Participial phrases* appear next to the word that they describe and are often set off from the rest of the sentence by a comma or by a set of commas.

   Calming his nerves by breathing slowly, Morris walked into the classroom to give a speech.

   Yvette, *always thinking quickly*, didn't even lose her place in the book.

   Disgusted after stopping twice for directions, I parked my car and hailed a cab.

   The bottle, *frozen solid*, had been left in the deep freeze all night.

REVIEW LISTS OF CONJUNCTIONS, TRANSITIONAL WORDS, RELATIVE PRONOUNS, AND PREPOSITIONS

The following *coordinating conjunctions* may be used to join words, phrases, or complete sentences:

and	but	for	nor
or	so	yet	

The following words and phrases are commonly used to show *transitions* between ideas:

therefore
thus } means *as a result*
consequently

however
nevertheless } mean *but*

furthermore } means *and*

then
finally } show a time relationship

The following *subordinating conjunctions* introduce dependent clauses:

after	as though	so (meaning *so that*)	until
although	because	so that	when
as	before	than	whenever
as if	even if	that	where
as long as	if	though	wherever
as soon as	since	unless	while

The following *relative pronouns* are commonly used to begin relative clauses:

that	who	whom	which	whose

Prepositional phrases begin with prepositions and end with nouns. The following are some common prepositions:

about	at	by	inside	onto	until
above	before	down	into	over	up
across	behind	during	like	since	upon
after	below	except	near	through	with
against	beneath	for	of	to	within
among	beside	from	off	toward	without
around	between	in	on	under	